Beyond the Winter Night

Elaine Brown

Christian Focus Publications

ISBN 1-85792-180-1

Published in 1995 by
Christian Focus Publications Ltd.
Geanies House, Fearn, Ross-shire,
IV20 1TW, Scotland, Great Britain.
Previously published by Kingsway.

Cover design by Donna Macleod

Contents

Preface

This small book was not easy to write, for death is a difficult subject to consider. Yet the needed thought and research offered me valuable learning experiences, several of which are described in coming pages.

Over recent months I have made new friends too, some of whom have been willing to share deep personal encounters with suffering and grief in order to help others struggling through similar circumstances. One or two names have been altered, but that is all.

Each chapter begins with a few quotations, followed by material from a diary kept in an attempt to record the sombre beauty of a northern winter. Unaware of any connection, I was keeping the diary at the same time as writing the book. Before long I realized that the certainty of coming spring was placing the difficult subject of death in a whole new light. A quite amazing light! I suddenly began to see with new eyes. The world around me was so magnificently illustrating that final climax, the triumph of God's life over evil and death.

Introduction

Allt Tuileach rises in the Grampian highlands of northern Scotland and tumbles eastwards, gathering streams as it goes. Soon the widening burn becomes the River Don, young and vigorous as it flows through the Strathdon farmlands. Much further on there is a place where, older and broader now, the river curves across a wide valley before reaching the last few hills and the sandy threshold of the North Sea. The Don's eighty-mile journey is over. Old age has led it into far more than the infant Allt Tuileach ever dreamed of.

Where the river curves across the wide valley there is a fast-growing village, the sudden change beginning when the oil boom burst upon this north-eastern corner during the 1970s. This is where we live, our home being on a small estate set beside the Don. In fact, the river runs close to our back fence, offering constant pleasure and interest. Beech woods line the further bank, and beyond fields and hills stretch into the distance. Bennachie strikes the skyline, one of its steep granite peaks – Mither Tap – rising above gentle rolling farmland. This is a magnificent part of the country!

Soon after moving in we discovered that all our immediate neighbours were newcomers like ourselves. Some had arrived from other parts of Britain, some from abroad, and a few from elsewhere in Scotland. One new friend was Calum. He was just out of school and starting work with an Aberdeenshire firm. Our chatting place was always the queue beside the ice-cream van. As soon as its horn blared down our street a row of front doors would open as neighbours dashed out. Most were children, so while they crowded around the counter choosing crisps and cones, Calum and I talked. He was shy and said little, but I always enjoyed his smile.

One damp November evening we bought our cones – five for our family and one each for him and his girlfriend – and hurried back to the warmth of our neighbouring homes.

'See you!' I called, pulling the heavy door shut with my foot.

'Aye!'

But we didn't see each other again. Five days later Calum died in an accident. I could hardly believe the news. Was Calum really gone! It seemed impossible. I couldn't take it in.

The small village kirk was almost full for the funeral, held on a bleak winter's afternoon as snowflakes drifted down out of a threatening sky. That day I felt the pain of Calum's death more deeply than ever. At dusk, when the ice-cream van came round, I missed him in the queue. I missed his smile.

The weeks and months passed. Winter became spring, and spring gave her own colourful welcome to coming summer. Everyone revelled in the brief, flower-scented warmth and then watched sadly as summer faded into gold, brown, and the final black of dying autumn. One November day I decided to wander through our village churchyard. The north wind was cold against my face and I could see another rain shower moving in across the fields. Damp confetti from the previous Saturday's wedding lay like sudden flowers among the turf-covered graves reminding me of how, even in the midst of joy, we are surrounded by death.

In fact, Calum's death had stirred me to ask deeper questions than had ever occurred to me before. And as I walked past the tall grey stones my questioning was accentuated by the sorrow of very many different bereavements. Parents had lost children in infancy or war, lonely partners had long outlived a husband or wife, large families had been tragically reduced by accident. That quiet country churchyard seemed to record so much of life.

I knew I would reach Calum's grave eventually. The roundabout route was deliberate. Every other memorial was unfamiliar, but Calum's was different. I felt very moved as I stood by the simple, granite stone which now marked his grave.

Why is there so much suffering and sorrow?
Where is Calum now?
Will we see each other again?

The questions kept playing on my mind. Then I
began deliberately to reassure myself. Death is not
a full stop. There *is* more than this here-and-now
world. A life beyond is promised by God, and only
then, within the wider context of eternity, will it
be possible for all our suffering and questioning
finally to be resolved.

That morning the certainty of 'more beyond
death' helped to relieve my bewilderment, and as
the dark November days passed I began to consider this all-important truth in more detail, aware
of its solemn significance as well as its strong comfort. Could such a truth transform even the sorrow
of bereavement? Or the anguish of terminal illness? Could it really prove to be a safe refuge?

1

LOSS THROUGH ACCIDENT

'I will see Joseph and my boys again!'

I can only say that it is honest to recognize a mystery and see inexplicable sorrow for what it is. Grief and groping are not sin ... God does not expect me to twist my mind to discover a pattern, where, too close to the tapestry I cannot yet trace it. (E. M. Blaiklock, *Kathleen: A Record of Sorrow*, page 38)

I believe in heaven. It makes sense of earth. (Len Barnett)

We seem to give them back to you O God who gave them to us. Not as the world gives do you give, O lover of men. For what you give you take not away .... Lift us up strong Son of God that we may see further .... Draw us closer to you that we may know ourselves to be closer to those we love. Prepare us also for that happy place, where with you (and with them) we may live for ever and ever. (attributed to Bede Jarett)

So we shall always be with the Lord. Therefore comfort one another with these words (1 Thessalonians 4:17-18 RSV).

November is particularly unwelcome here in the north-east. It drags us unwillingly towards winter, and sometimes the first fierce blizzard will blow in across the hills before the month is over. But a few November days are beautiful, and valued the more because of their rarity.

There was one sunlit Sunday when the dull, granite wall around the churchyard suddenly glistened as if set with a thousand diamonds. It was my turn on the door duty at Morning Service and, standing there by the little-used side entrance of the kirk, I could gaze over the wall and across to the nine young lime trees beyond. What an exquisite tracery their thin branches made against the gleaming sky! Aberdeenshire 'beef-on-the-hoof' grazed close to the farmstead and up on the nearby hill noisy crows flocked newly-ploughed furrows. But there was no other sound, not even a footstep on the gravel path. Door duty at the side entrance always offered plenty of opportunity for undisturbed reflection.

After a little while I began to wander down the path enjoying the clear, cold sunlight. Close against the sparkling wall I noticed a small memorial stone and paused to glance at the inscription. Immediately the words gripped me – a father of thirty-six years and his twin sons of five 'drowned on 4th Sept. 1965.'

It was the kind of inscription you can't get out

of your mind. I thought about the family for a long time afterwards, trying to imagine what such a loss must have meant to a young mother. How had the accident occurred? What had happened in the years since? How had she coped? A few weeks later, when talking with our village undertaker, I asked if he still remembered that autumn day when the funeral took place.

'Yes, I remember it well,' he said. 'It was a remarkable funeral. So much singing, even in the churchyard. Quite different from other quiet, solemn services. There was such a sense of triumph in the church that day, even though it was a tragedy. I think those people must have had great faith.'

I knew then that the young widow must still have found God to be a refuge even in her intense sorrow, and I longed to be able to meet and talk with her.

'She didn't come from the village,' the undertaker told me. 'But friends here arranged the burial because costs are cheaper in the country.'

It was through those same friends that I discovered more about the family. What an unusual story! The husband, Joseph, arrived in Scotland from the Ukraine during the Second World War. He was in his late teens then – a handsome, dark-haired fellow, who through much personal hardship in eastern Europe had been drawn to Jesus Christ and had given over his young life to him. Joseph was

posted to a work camp near the village here and
before long began searching for Christian friends
in the area. That was how he met the older, local
couple who were soon to become so important to
him. They welcomed him as their own son, and
later, when Joseph met his attractive English bride,
Edna, they included her in the warmth of their family circle. This meant so much to Joseph, for he
had lost all contact with his own relatives in the
Ukraine, not even knowing if they were still alive.

In time Joseph trained as a hairdresser and set
up his own small business in Aberdeen. The couple moved into a council flat in the city and after a
while their first daughter, Olwyn, was born. Life
became even more busy when the twins, Martyn
and Mark, arrived three years later, but by that time
the family had made friends at their local Brethren fellowship, and baby-minders were in plenti-
ful supply. Four years passed and then, to their
amazement, the fourth baby Joseph and Edna were
expecting turned out to be another set of twins – a
boy and a girl! What excitement! Joseph felt so
proud of his five small children. They more than
made up for the loneliness he had experienced after being forcibly separated from his own family.

Despite the busy demands of each day, that upstairs flat was quite often full of laughter and fun,
and when friends called on Joseph and Edna they
felt drawn by the warmth and caring of their home.

Of course it was hard to be cooped up in so small
a space, and it was difficult to live with the constant uncertainties of a limited income. Joseph and
Edna regularly made a point of putting their situation into God's hands, and it reassured them to
know that, in this way, they could hand themselves
over to someone so much stronger.

On that stormy Saturday morning they started
the day as usual by asking for God's keeping and
strength, and then busy weekend activities began.
I will let Edna tell their story now, as she told it to
me just last week, when we met:

'That day remains as clear in my mind as if it
was only yesterday. Joseph had been concerned
about helping a young lad who didn't yet know
Jesus. He'd often prayed about the boy and was
planning to share some Bible verses with him that
Saturday evening, but first of all he took Martyn
and Mark fishing. They must have driven down
the coast a short distance, looking for a sheltered
cove. I stayed at home because the twins were so
small then. Olwyn stayed with me, too. Halfway
through the afternoon something strange happened. It was as if my heart suddenly turned over.
Do you know the feeling? Well, that was what happened – just for a split-second. Then I forgot about
it. The babies and Olwyn kept me busy that wet,
windy afternoon.

'After a while the doorbell rang. A policeman

was standing outside our small upstairs flat. He asked if Joseph was at home. I told him that he'd be in later. Then I said, 'Has Joseph done anything with the car?' (He always had difficulty driving.) But the policeman answered, 'No!' and went away. I closed the door and didn't think any more about the matter. I just thought 'Joseph will be home by six!' and then went back to the babies.

'But later, around teatime, the policeman came back. He told me that Joseph and the boys were missing, that a high wave had perhaps swept over the rock where they were fishing together. The car had been found on a road quite close by. A search had begun.

'I just couldn't take it in. I couldn't at all. While the policeman was talking to me the babies began to cry. They were hungry. So I said, "I've got to go and give the children their tea," and excused myself. There was so much to do. I just carried on in a mechanical kind of way but it was like walking through a strange, bewildering dream. Nothing seemed real at all. I only remembered that feeling I'd had earlier in the afternoon and I knew it must have been at the time the wave came.

'A friend came to stay with me straight away. That was a great help. We shared all the work together. The work was what kept me going. I needed to be busy. Carrying on with the children's routine was important. Life had to go on. I found I couldn't read the Bible or pray for about three days after the accident. I was so stunned that nothing would go in. But then I came across the first verse of Isaiah chapter 43: *'Fear not, for I have redeemed you; I have called you by name, you are mine'* (RSV). Those words helped me so much. I kept thinking of them. There was also a verse on my kitchen calendar: *'He shall carry them (the lambs) in his bosom'* (Isaiah 40:11 AV). It was really lovely to keep seeing those words. They comforted me.

'People were very good in those first few days. They kept coming to see us and taking care of our needs. But then, quite suddenly, many of them just stopped calling. I felt really hurt about that. I couldn't understand it. But one friend came regularly for months and months after the accident. Almost every day. She would sit, read and pray with me and it was a tremendous help. I could relax and listen, and afterwards I felt better. It refreshed me.

' There was something else which I will never forget. It was the way in which all the Assemblies in this area rallied round to help financially. When Joseph died we had just £200. That was all. £200. We'd never had much of an income from his small gent's hairdressing business. We didn't worry about it because we never seemed to need more. But when Joseph died all our Brethren friends collected a gift. It came to £1,500. I was amazed! It was such a big amount for that time. I used £12 per week for family needs and invested the rest. I never guessed that it would last us for six years!

'But then, in those early days, I couldn't think ahead to the future at all. I lived every day as it came. My mind refused to go further. At first there was the awful suspense of the search. It went on and on, but they didn't find Joseph or the boys. Then, two weeks later, on the very day my other twins were a year old, one of the little boys was found. A Brethren fishing crew discovered his body in their net when they hauled it in. Wasn't it amazing how God caused that to happen? The other little boy was never found.

'But worrying about Joseph was worst of all. He was such a good swimmer. I couldn't believe that he'd drowned. "He must be alive somewhere!" I kept telling myself, and then I thought of all the coves along that part of the coast just south of Aberdeen. I felt sure he must still be there.

'I went down to England to visit my parents and it was on my mind all the time. When I was driving those long miles back to Aberdeen I kept on asking God to help them find my husband. They found his body that same evening. It was six weeks after the accident. I think it was then that the loss suddenly became real to me. I knew that Joseph had died, and that now we were alone. It was very hard. I needed my friend very much more then.

When she came to read and pray with me I needed her support more than ever.

'What tore me apart most of all, even then, was wondering if they had suffered. It kept playing on my mind. I think it would have been quick for the little boys, but what about Joseph? Being a good swimmer, he would have struggled to reach his boys. It must have been so awful for him. I thought about it many times. In the end God had to take that fear from me. I knew that Joseph and the boys were with him and that all their suffering was now over. And so the fears started to fade.

'The other thing which tore me apart was having to sort out the little boys' clothes and give them away. That was awful. I also gave all of Joseph's things away. Immediately. His clothes went to friends, and so on. I got rid of all his books too. I should never have done that. It was a mistake. Later I began to wish I still had Joseph's books. Maybe the children would have liked them? Now I always tell people not to give everything away. Wait. Shut the door of the room or cupboard, and wait. Even six months. It's better that way. I've always regretted not waiting.

'I suppose I sorted everything out straight away because I wanted to keep busy. I never remember feeling worn out. Some people are surprised when I say that, but I have a great capacity for hard work. I've always been like that. Of course, I missed

Joseph's help terribly. He was wonderful with the children and helped with them, especially after the second two babies were born. I was very ill then, but Joseph made it easier for me. It wasn't the norm for Ukrainian husbands to help with the home and family. The custom is for them to sit down when they get in from work, and let the women do everything. But Joseph wasn't like that at all.

'The loss hit me hardest in the evenings when there wasn't so much to do, and the children were fast asleep. I would think, "Just a few weeks ago there were seven of us, and now we're only four." It hurt me deeply when I thought of it like that. Then the weekends were difficult too. That was the time when Joseph would have been home with us all. Maybe we'd have taken a picnic to the park or sea front. Now it was difficult to do that alone. Sad, somehow. Of course, I did sometimes make the effort and take the three little ones out, but it wasn't the same. For the first few months I never went out at all in the evenings. I couldn't leave the babies. Mind you, I didn't let my sorrow show, for the children's sakes, especially Olwyn. I never cried in front of the children. Never. Except for maybe a quick tear. I didn't want to make them upset.

Olwyn had been very close to her father. He was so thrilled when she was born. "I've got a daughter of my own!" he kept saying over and over again. He longed to contact his mother and tell

her the news, but no one knew where she was.
Joseph played the accordion and when Olwyn grew
bigger he taught her the piano so that they could
play together. She loved it! But after her father died
she stopped playing completely for a year or more.
She seemed to close up and wouldn't talk about
her daddy. I think the loss had an adverse effect on
her for a very long time afterwards. She never did
well at school even though she was quite bright. It
seemed as if the shock of losing her father had
affected her learning.

'As time went by I think I began to accept what
had happened a little more. I suppose we got into
some sort of routine at last, and that helped. I found
it hard living in an upstairs flat, so asked the Council for a move, and that was when they gave us the
house. It was really lovely! It had a big garden too.
The children could play outside, and I felt much
better. I think that move helped me to get over my
sorrow a little more.

'Of course, I couldn't go out to work – I'm a
nurse – but I managed to do an evening course in
book-keeping. At the time I didn't know why I was
choosing that particular subject but it appealed.
Then when the invested money ran out, I knew I
must look for work. I went to visit a friend – she'd
invited me over – and when I arrived she offered
me a job. As warden of the YWCA hostel in the
city! She knew I was a nurse but "I'm afraid you'll

need some book-keeping training too," she said.
When I told her I'd just been to those evening
classes she was amazed. Wasn't it wonderful how
God planned that? It was his way of getting me
ready for the new job.

'So we moved from our house and went to live
at the hostel. I had forty girls to look after, as well
as all the staff. It was a busy, happy time for me.
We were part of a big family and that made a great
difference.

'Many years have gone by since then! Looking
back I think that the hardest part of all has been
not having someone to share with me in bringing
up our three children. There have been so many
times when I just longed for Joseph's help. He was
such a strong, supportive person. Together we could
have decided on the right thing to do. But without
him I often wondered if I was taking the wisest
course of action. There's no one to check with. You
have to make all the decisions alone, pay all the
bills, and so on.

'I know now that I spoiled the children too
much. I was afraid they'd be badly affected by losing their father, so I tried to make up for their loneliness by always including other children in the
things we did together at home. We took them with
us on outings, too. There were always other children around. I encouraged them. But it meant that
we rarely spent time alone as a family. I never had

a chance to get close to my own three, especially Olwyn. I regret that now.

'There's something else which comes straight to my mind when I look back. I know that the hope I have in God has made all the difference in my loss. I will see Joseph and my boys again! Some people believe that when you die it's the end. Like falling asleep and never waking up. I can't understand how they can believe that. I just can't. It doesn't make sense. But heaven does. One day I shall look back and understand, but that won't be yet. Not, perhaps, until I reach heaven too.

'It's true — the Lord's people never really die. They just go on to a better life, because in giving themselves fully to him they've become one with him for always. That truth seemed to burn like a fire inside Joseph. He knew he must bring others – like the young lad that Saturday – to Jesus Christ so that they could live for ever too. He couldn't bear his friends not to know the relief of forgiveness and then the lovely certainty of heaven.

'Remembering this, I deliberately chose one of Joseph's favourite Bible promises for his grave, John 11:26 (AV): Whosoever *liveth and believeth in me (God) shall never die. It*'s true. It really is! And it's tremendously exciting too. Imagine it! Everybody who belongs to Jesus will live for ever with him, in joy! This truth has been very important to me and very reassuring, even recently.

'Not long ago – just three years – I married again. My second husband was a widower who'd been a family friend for years. At first I was hesitant about remarriage, but then I knew it was right and so we all moved down to England. My husband had bought a lovely bungalow near the coast and it made me happy to feel that, now my children were growing older, I'd still have someone to care for. Caring for people has always been important to me, particularly since Joseph's death.

'But, on the evening of our wedding day, my husband was suddenly taken ill. He'd had a bad heart for some time and I knew he wasn't fit. Thirteen days later he died. All the previous deep sorrows suddenly surfaced again and the pain was very acute.

'I knew I must ease my sadness by reaching out to others and helping them. That was what had made all the difference before. After a while (I didn't hurry this time) I told the twins I wanted to sell the bungalow and buy a larger house so that I could open a home for elderly people who were lonely and needed care. They agreed, and that's how my whole new 'family' has now come into being!

'Not that the move has been easy. Far from it. Sometimes the obstacles, particularly in the financial line, have been all but overwhelming. Sometimes I've had big doubts about the whole idea.

But they haven't lasted long. I've felt the Lord close to me even at the hardest, most puzzling times and somehow (maybe only he knows how!) we opened the front door to our first residents just seven months ago.

'Helping others continues to be important to me. I remember that years ago when I was alone and the twins were still babies, I used to sit down and pray for other people. Some evenings I would pray for hours and hours. And then I found I could help in practical ways too. I started going to a sewing group and doing different things like that. Looking back, those evenings of prayer were amongst the most precious experiences of my life. I can honestly say that. As I reached out to others the Lord gave me his serenity. He really did. And he still does. It's wonderful. I never thought it could happen. Not out of such grief and darkness . . .'

There were tears in Edna's eyes as she finished speaking but that same triumph, evident all those long years ago at the funeral, was still there. Still strong. Through her sorrow Edna had taken refuge in God and found him to be completely trustworthy. She could not yet fully trace the pattern he was weaving through her life, but that had not given her any cause to doubt his wisdom or love. In fact, as she put it, 'the Lord has become increasingly real to me because I've needed him so much!'

And, more than all else, the darkness of her sorrow has been shot through with a strong shaft of hope. As Edna herself said, speaking through her tears, 'Joseph and my boys are already there in heaven. One day I shall join them, and then we'll be always together. The long sadness will be over at last.'

Chapter Two

The loss of a marriage partner

'How ever will I cope?'

I am sure it is never sadness – a proper, straight, natural response to loss – that does people harm, but all the other things, all the resentment, dismay, doubt, and self-pity with which it is usually complicated. Be careful of your own bodily health .... You must remain, as she wishes, a good instrument for all heavenly impulses to work upon. (C. S. Lewis, writing to a widower, in *A Severe Mercy*)

Widowhood, like any kind of living, required a faith that would cost me everything. I had to let go of all former securities and strengths to find the new securities God had for me. (Katie F. Wiebe, *Alone*)

If his comfort were limited to pity or commiserating with us it would lead us to self-pity, and that's no help at all. Rather, the Spirit's comfort puts courage into us, empowers us to cope ... it is a strong, courageous word, equal to every sorrow and perplexity and disappointment. (Catherine Marshall, *The Helper*)

Fear not, for I am with you, be not dismayed, for I am your God; I will strengthen you, I will help you, I will uphold you with my victorious right hand. (Isaiah 41:10 RSV).

Winter has closed in. This year it seems the more unwelcome and difficult because my husband has just left for six months of flying work abroad. Six weeks have passed. There are eighteen more to go. Loneliness is acute at times, particularly late in the evening. The emptiness is real, though it is by no means permanent. He *will* be back!

Most of the day I am numb to the effects of his going. There is plenty to lead my thoughts away in other directions. But then, late at night, the loneliness swamps me. No voice; no touch; no warm, familiar partner to delight in. It feels like some kind of pain deep in an inaccessible place. And I try to push it aside, afraid lest I should become self-pitying.

Sleep comes, numbing reality again. And I sleep well too. A deep sleep, full of strange, vivid dreams. The new day brings new activity, plans, responsibilities. I do not feel the emptiness as morning creeps in through the window. Only when some small detail loosens a rush of memories – seeing his work-boots down in the hall ready for use, or the black cossack hat on the stand ...

No, he hasn't gone for ever. He will be back. And meanwhile I wait, filling each day with activity, determined to cope. But what if the water pipes freeze? (Last week the temperature dropped to -20 degrees C.) What if the washing machine packs up again as it did last summer? What if one

of those complicated tax forms arrives? What if
one of the twins has an accident on his bike?
(They've come so close to it already.) What if ...?

Some days I feel full of confidence, proud to
be managing the household so well. At other times
it's quite different. On such occasions I've usually
begun the day feeling empty and sad, then edgy
and apprehensive. The slightest hitch or problem
appears huge and threatening. I worry for hours,
imagining all kinds of likely developments, each
more alarming than the last. And then, suddenly
and easily the problem resolves itself, and I begin
to smile a little at myself.

Or maybe a baffling difficulty actually does occur. (There really was a complicated financial
query last week.) And because I'm already feeling discouraged the whole thing swamps me. I can't
think straight, nor reason the matter out. My tired
mind begins to spin. If only my husband were here
to offer a cool, collected answer. If only he hadn't
had to go away. How will we manage through the
rest of this long winter? How am I going to cope?

These are the fears which have been playing
through my mind recently. There have been moments when, acutely aware of my own limitations,
I have gone up to our bedroom (it overlooks the
calm murmuring river) and knelt at the bed, plead-
ing for God's help. It has taken a while for my tense
body to relax and my restless mind to become still,

but at last the peace has come and I have gone back into the day feeling reassured, aware that I am not alone after all. God does take my hand. He does lead me through the long, demanding days. If I will let him.

This is proving to be an exacting but valuable learning experience for me during these weeks when I feel my husband's absence so keenly. Yet he is only away for a temporary period. How very much harder it must be for those who have been bereaved of a partner. While Edna was speaking of her experiences I began to glimpse something of what such a loss must mean. I found myself feeling with her. Edna's focus now is largely upon the future, the delight of one day being with her husband and sons in the completeness and permanence of heaven.

But, in looking back, she also spoke of her need to constantly depend upon God throughout the long, difficult years since the accident. She knew that in giving herself fully to God she had become closely one with God, through Jesus, and so could never really be alone. But nonetheless she often struggled with an acute sense of incompleteness. The bewilderment is inevitable, for a grieving partner feels as if half of his very person has gone. It has been described in this way:

I was wrong to say that the stump was recovering from the pain of amputation ... it has so many ways to hurt me that I discover them only one by one (C. S. Lewis, *A Grief Observed*).

The hurt is deep and real, and because the incompleteness will always remain 'there is only the skilled and more skilled covering of the wound .... The task is one of courage, faith, will to conquer. It is like the task of the disabled .... There is no healing, only victory to pursue. (E. M. Blaiklock, *Kathleen: A Record of Sorrow*).

At first sight that statement only seems to underline the feeling of helplessness. A bereaved partner hardly knows where to begin. 'Only victory to pursue.' But how? The victory comes not so much in a moment of once-and-for-all triumph as in a repeated turning to God. A repeated awareness of our dependence. This dependence will occasionally find conscious expression in a period of calm resting, but much more often it is only realized when circumstances have become all but overwhelming. It is when we have reached the very end of ourselves and suddenly realize that his right hand is yet holding us. Then we are able gradually to relax. To affirm our dependence again, and so slowly to draw on new strength. It is the valuable outworking of close personal oneness with God.

A young widow, June, has spoken of this. She wrote a long letter recently in which she described many different aspects of her bereavement. Some must have been hard to express on paper and yet she wanted to share in this way so that others might be encouraged and helped. This is how she described her experiences, and her awareness of God *'upholding her with his victorious right hand.'* I will share the entire letter because there is so much of value in it:

'It is nearly four years since Andrew died from that sudden heart attack. The experience has been devastating and yet God has still kept us, still cared for us. I have been reminded of this over and over again. People said the first year would be the worst. I'm not sure that I agree. During the early weeks and months numbness acted as a shock-absorber and friends were supportive, even sympathetic if a sudden burst of tears caught me "on the hop" without warning.

'Then the numbness began to wear off. Two things brought me face to face with reality. One was the pain of realizing that "you just aren't supposed to be widowed so young" and the other was an urgent (and unforeseen) financial need. Andrew thought he had made good material provision for us, but this proved not to be the case. I now recognize our need of an income as clear evidence of God's hand being on our circumstances, for he was helping me to move out in trust and discover the new plans he had made for us.

'All kinds of changes occurred when after a few weeks I began full-time work. I had to discipline myself, making an effort to look smart, even attractive, first thing in the morning. Then too, things like shopping, washing, and ironing all had to be organized each day. Life suddenly became very full but it was worth it, for in my new, responsible employment I gradually began to feel needed. There was a particular contribution I had to make. This proved essential to my morale. It was another way in which God was beginning to help me out of my sorrow.

'My new role had forced me into a regular routine at the home end. I had to prepare proper meals again and so on. Then too, Peter and Linda still needed caring for, so I had to bother for their sakes. I also made myself bother about the upkeep of the house. It was a case of summoning up willpower and deliberately getting on with the redecorating Andrew had planned to do. When at last I reached the hall and staircase I remembered two friends through whom God had already helped me. They are the sort of people who are genuinely glad to assist with anything. So I swallowed my pride and asked if they could take over. They did. And they also valiantly helped with redecorating the lounge. Why do I tell you all this? Because it is part of the way the Lord keeps his promise of special care for the "widow and fatherless". He does enable, I know!

'Of course there are still times when I miss Andrew terribly, perhaps more now after four years than I did at first when Peter and Linda made more demands on me. The emotional side is hardest of all. I can't expect to spend nearly eighteen years working to make a marriage happy and successful – welding two lives into one – without feeling completely lost when that one is cut in half, leaving behind an open, tender wound. Our intimate life together had been so very happy and precious, yet suddenly this loving special togetherness was no longer my privilege. I have never felt able to talk to anyone about this. Perhaps it is also an aspect of my bereavement with which I have yet to ask directly for God's help. The very fact of admitting it now may well be a release. I should have shared my emptiness before.

'Not that I have had much opportunity lately for such sharing. Inevitably, as time has gone by, friends have stopped calling in. Sometimes I feel very hurt when people forget that I still long for friendship and fellowship. There is a deep need to pray with others too, just as Andrew and I used to do together. In fact it is needed more than ever now. But prayer is usually an 'alone' experience.

'I admit there are also times when I cannot pray,

often because I'm terribly tired. (I try to overcome
this difficulty by having a prayer time halfway
through each evening, rather than waiting until
bedtime.) During the night there are many wake-
ful hours. I find this trying, for much as I long to
sleep, I can't. I've attempted to make some use of
this time instead, but so far without any real suc-
cess. Yet, despite all, my faith in God continues to
be very real. It definitely keeps me going!

'There's often a need to check myself out on
the matter of bitterness. I've particularly needed
God's help with this. It's quite a struggle. I felt
bitter when Peter and Linda were trying to get to
grips with O-level revision and I was quite unable
to help. Andrew's assistance would have been in-
valuable with that ever difficult subject, maths. But
the two of them passed their exams when the time
came, so all was well.

'Feeling hurt is, perhaps, a part of bitterness. I
felt hurt when, after approaching two men at our
church about helping Peter to drive, both said they
were too busy. Peter is eighteen now and has been
driving for over a year, so we've coped with that
one, and I expect we'll teach Linda as well when
she's old enough. It's just that I don't feel Mum is
the best person to teach a teenage lad to drive nor,
come to that, to talk to him about the things that
matter in life. Sometimes Peter desperately needs a
father-figure.

'In a quite different way Linda needed lots and lots of loving patience and understanding when her daddy died, but this poem really encouraged me. She wrote it quite spontaneously and I haven't altered a single word:

> *One day*
> *You and I*
> *Will once more*
> *Share the same world.*
> *Yours is the name*
> *That should be remembered,*
> *Loved, and cherished.*
> *By all, not just by me.*
> *I will try to carry on*
> *Where your modesty left you.*
> *And try to create a legend*
> *For us both*
> *For us all.*

'Incidentally, I'd hate to give the impression that things are always hard and gloomy. That's certainly not the case. True, I did once wonder if I'd ever be able to laugh or sing again, but I can and do. The three of us have lots of good giggles together, just as we did when Andrew was with us.

'I realize that these times of fun and pleasure centre entirely around our small family now, whereas once Andrew and I used also to enjoy regu-

lar evenings out and a good laugh with our friends.
Since Andrew died my social life has become non-
existent. I've looked at this hard and long, and have
come to the conclusion that a young widow is seen
as a threat by other women, even Christians. I once
confessed to a church member that I enjoyed mas-
culine company and she was horrified. Later I
wished I hadn't thought of such honesty. On another occasion, when wearing a new dress to
church, a married lady remarked, "You look nice!
Whose husband are you after?"

'It is small wonder that I've become defensive
in my relationships. I feel I must be. At least, for
the present. This is another area where God may
well help things to be different later on. (I find
that some things *have* to be "left pending" in this
long programme of re-adjustment. God will bring
me to them eventually, when I am more ready.)

'The present lack of much outside company has
meant that my life inevitably centres around Peter
and Linda. But they are growing up. Soon they
will have their own lives to live, their own career
ideas and plans to fulfil. God is helping me to see
that a deliberate new pattern of thinking is already
needed. It's a discipline. I know that I must *not*
think, "Peter and Linda don't need me any more"
but "Now Peter and Linda are growing up I can
enjoy some of my own activities, even go away for
a weekend and leave them to look after them-

selves." I must *not* think, "Now I'm all alone" *but* "Now I'm able to be almost independent too!"

For much of the time I can keep my mind focused ahead like that, at least until a special occasion like our anniversary comes along. Then it's hard. I confess that when friends celebrate their Silver Weddings it hurts. It hurts terribly. But I've also seen God's tenderness to me, through others, on my own anniversaries. A dear elderly friend sends me a loving note on Andrew's birthday, our wedding anniversary and Andrew's "heavenly birthday". It is a welcome reminder that someone does care on such empty days.

'I have other friends – a married couple – to whom I've been able to turn for particular help. They've advised about money, income tax, budgeting, careers for Peter and Linda, etc. I can never thank them adequately for the loving care they continue to show. I often feel grateful to God for them. I also have a near neighbour, a widow, with whom I can share outings or an occasional weekend away. We pray with one another about our respective children and this is a real help. Thank you, Lord, for Mary!

'Looking back over these years I am so grateful that I have no "if onlys" to mourn over. We always made sure that if were impatient, intolerant or horrid to one another, it was put right before we went to bed. So there are no "if onlys". Andrew loved us all so much. I'm glad that, in dying suddenly, he didn't have time to be anxious about us. He was proud of Peter and Linda and was a wonderful dad. They have only happy memories – something else to be very grateful for.

'Before Andrew died I had never seen death. I'd never talked about it, and avoided meeting the bereaved. Not any more. I know how it feels to be avoided. I was not encouraged to talk about Andrew, but talking is important. I now encourage folk in similar circumstances to speak about how they're feeling, show me photographs, etc., as they feel they want to. I believe that all these experiences in our lives can be used as a way of helping others and I'm willing to do this.

'It is true. The Lord *does* have a special caring for the widow and fatherless and I urge them to claim his promise and live by it. It works!'

I was moved by June's letter. Her honesty drew me to her and deepened the bond between us. The pain of loss is still there but it has been comforted by the "skilled and more skilled covering of the wound". How wise and understanding is the God who constantly tends us in our need, taking up our helplessness into his strength!

There is something very compelling about such caring and love. How much closer we are drawn to God through adversity! I am discovering this within my own far smaller difficulty, and June has found it to be true in hers. Does God use even adversity to make us feel our need of him the more? Offering us an unexpected richness just when we thought we had lost most? It is a mystery. Hard to recognize, particularly when you are at the turmoiled centre of a sorrowing storm. But the more I've thought about it, the more I've realized it to be true.

God is never more vital and dear to us than at the moment when we fully sense our helplessness and need. That is how we first come to him, aware of the wrong within us, and longing to be forgiven and put right. And this is how we discover him again and again in all the bewildering events which may follow. Only he can make our deepest sorrow still to hold value. Only he can bring the first shaft of light out of darkness, the first touch of calm out of turmoil, the first promise of joy out of pain. Nor docs he wait until we enter into eternity. He delights to enrich us now.

Chapter Three

The loss of a baby

'Can I still trust God?'

Mysteries remain, but to those who hold the faith ... they are now mysteries of light and not of darkness. And that is true even of the final mysteries of suffering and death. (Sir Thomas Taylor)

Faith is willingness to trust God when the pieces don't fit, as well as willingness to trust when life moves steadily along, as it will. (Katie F. Wiebe, *Alone*)

Faith is weakness hanging on to strength. (Bishop Festo Kivengere)

The Lord is good. When trouble comes, he is the place to go! And he knows everyone who trusts in him! (Nahum 1:7 TLB)

There was such a calm across the beech woods this morning. As I shook the sheepskin rug out of our bedroom window I paused to drink in the quiet loveliness of it all, delighting in the steady on-flow of the river.

Then, at midday, a blizzard burst in across the hills. It came completely without warning, forcing the bare black trees to bend in submission. Soon thick snowflakes were clinging to their empty branches – an intricate collage of white. By then I could hardly see beyond the nearer beeches – so instead I stood by the window looking up into the gloomy sky, watching the thick speckling of flakes fall towards the frozen river bank and the restless grey water. There were no familiar crows or gulls in sight, no heron fishing from that favourite down-stream rock, no golden-eye ducks diving deep beneath the river's rough surface. The world outside seemed suddenly lifeless, except for the menacing wind and the frantic snowflakes.

By supper time the fall was nearly two feet deep, drifting up against our wall. I remembered how hard it was to push the front door open last winter. And how heavy avalanches of snow slid stealthily off the overhanging eaves just when we were briefly negotiating the front step beneath. Winter here is magnificent and irritating, exciting and tedious. So bewildering a mixture! And at present almost all of it lies ahead.

This afternoon, as I looked out at the twilight sky (the snow was still splatting against our windows) I couldn't help yearning to be far away where the sun is hot and the world ablaze with colour. My mind inevitably went back to other January days, spent in Ethiopia, where we worked for a few years. I remembered how that month was one of the hottest in the whole year.

Sometimes we took a holiday in January, staying at a mission guest house which lay nestled in the steep tree-covered hillside above a small crater lake. It was idyllic! How we revelled in the hot tropical sunshine sparkling over the cold blue water, and in the single shaft of moonlight which fell across the lake when black night crept in!

That secluded setting is full of extra-happy memories for our family. I thought of them this afternoon, reliving our enjoyment. But then I remembered our final January in Ethiopia. That year it was different. It is hard to recall the experience of that holiday, and the months which followed. But if, in doing so, I can draw alongside other mothers who have known a similar sorrow, then the sharing will have been worthwhile.

I am very aware that, in losing an unborn baby, my own experience of loss was only a faint shadow of the sorrow which many others have had to face, and yet, to me, it was overwhelming. (How much harder it must be for a mother to lose a baby she has known and cared for.) Other parents who have been through a similar grief will understand, knowing what it is like to be full of joyous anticipation at the promise of a child, and then suddenly to find that the baby has died. In that moment of bitter realization a mother feels robbed of all the thrill of making plans and preparations. There is nothing left but the deep raw pain of loss. A miscarriage or stillbirth is a very real bereavement. A mother who has lost her unborn child may feel bereft of a deep part of herself. That was the anguish I knew.

It was not our first baby, but our fourth. 'Then why grieve so much?' people might have asked. But they didn't know of the prolonged and frustrating physical difficulties I had encountered since the birth of our youngest children – six-year-old twin boys. Nor could they have known that this unusual hormone imbalance might well be relieved by the birth of another baby, were that ever to prove possible. No one, except perhaps my husband, could have guessed at the immense joy I felt when I was found I was going to have another child. I was elated! That baby was particularly dear to me. Its birth promised to fulfil so many deep hopes.

The twelfth week came and went. 'That's like passing a milestone. Everything should go well from now on!' I was told, and so I started to put all my eager plans into immediate action. There was so much to do and such pleasure in doing it.

'At last our January holiday came and we set off excitedly for the guest house. The children couldn't wait to swim, sail and fish from the rowing boat. I was looking forward to a favourite hilltop walk which would take us right around the lake, offering the pleasure of colourful birds and wild flowers en route. And we weren't disappointed! That first week was as full and happy as we'd anticipated! Late each evening my husband and I walked down to the small jetty which led out into the lake and, pausing in the moonlit silence, I would think ahead into the coming months, feeling a great excitement and joy.

Saturday came. Early that evening I suddenly knew that something was wrong. A wretched, desperate realization, filling me with dread. I remember that I lay on our bed in the small wooden chalet seeing the night breeze play through the cotton curtains, and hearing the strange rasping rhythm of cicadas in the grass outside. It was another twilight, another calm ending to the day, but this time I couldn't take any of it in. My mind was too full of fear. I remember my husband searching for the ignition keys and then taking me down the path to our car while friends put our three children to bed. I hated going away and leaving them. I hated the drive down the rough dusty track, away into the black night. And most of all I hated the pain. I couldn't believe it was happening.

It seemed a long time before we reached Addis Ababa but the distance was only about thirty miles. I was trying to doze when my husband announced, 'I can see the city lights!' and a few miles further on we reached the hospital. A strange echoing place, cold and unwelcoming. I remember that my husband had to leave around 11 pm. It was important for him to return to our children. Our kind doctor visited, and then the small, unfamiliar room was dark.

There was no sound at all, except for the distant rumble of traffic and the noise of stray dogs barking in the streets close by. I must have slept for a while, waking just as the first pale glow of dawn was breaking over the further hills. I could see tall fir trees beyond the window, outlined against the grey sky, intricate and beautiful.

I lay staring at them for a long time, following the pattern of each branch, and in the freshness of a new morning trying to forget my apprehension. But it could not be forgotten. The pain had returned, each sharp stab leaving me tense with dread. It couldn't be happening. I had so longed for this child. All my thoughts and plans had centred around the baby's arrival – weeks, months ahead. But the birth must not be yet, it was far too early. The baby would die. I refused to even let that last word linger in my mind.

The first few golden strands of day began to stretch far out across the sky. I watched as they drew closer, slanting down through the trees, and as I watched I began to plead with God asking him to keep the child well and strong. Surely he would? God wouldn't allow anything to endanger the life he had so remarkably given to us! Reminding myself of this, I was reassured, but even so dared not think further about the future. Once or twice my mind began to visualize the room we had been preparing, and the clothes carefully laid out on a cupboard shelf. But then I quickly shut the pictures away. I couldn't cope with it.

For a while the pain eased and I began to be full of hope. 'It's over now!' I decided, and let myself enjoy the warm sunlight flooding in across the small grey room. I think that very confidence made the next stab of pain all the more bewildering. I wanted to yell out, 'No, no, it can't be! It mustn't be!' But I didn't break the silence of that empty room. I only felt the rush of tears. The pain intensified, each thrust more strong and frequent. I hated the whole experience; I grew angry and frustrated as the hot sun rose high in the sky. Years before I had welcomed such pain and felt the thrill of bringing a child into the world. Now I resented it, objecting to its intrusion. I fought it, refusing to accept what was happening.

The rest of that morning remains indistinct –

the nurses, the kindly doctor, painkillers, the talk of tests. And then the sudden dreaded climax. The birth and the death, all one. Everyone was kind and tender. They spoke softly and made me comfortable between the stiff white sheets. Then they went quietly away.

In those few moments before my husband came the huge pent-up storm broke. I couldn't believe it. I just couldn't. How could I have been happily choosing names one day and then suddenly not needing one of them the next? How could I have been daily delighting in the early stir of new life, only to find it stilled and gone in the space of hours? It seemed impossible. It couldn't have happened. But it had.

I asked to see the baby. He was tiny and complete. There was something awesome about gazing down at such miniature perfection, knowing it to have been God's making within me. God's intricate, unseen work, but still and lifeless now. In those moments of silence, I felt the first faint stir of wonder. I think I began to worship God despite my grief.

A few days passed. I was home again. 'Mummy won't be having a baby now,' my husband had explained to our small family. I thrust myself back into the usual routine and worked my way down a list of quite unnecessary tasks. The house began to gleam. One day I put all the baby clothes in a cardboard carton and sent them away to a children's home. Another day I sat out on our sunny porch and completed the last baby jacket. I decided to give it to a friend. Her baby was almost due. The lonely days slipped by.

I was forcing myself to be busy, but the nights were bleak. I would pretend to be settling down in bed but I was wide awake, listening until my husband's steady even breathing told me he was asleep. Then I would get up and creep along the stone-tiled floor to the living room. I would read, write, try to pray or just sit feeling utterly spent. The numbness which had shielded me all day wore off during those long night hours. It was then that the pain throbbed, that grief tore me apart. I couldn't bear it. Would I ever be able to accept what had happened? Would this sorrowing ever cease?

I remember the moment, in the silent early hours of a dark morning, when I came to the very end of my endurance. I knew I could not cope any longer. I had reached the cold hard rock at the bottom of despair. There was only one reasonable alternative left. I could not go further down. I could only reach very hesitantly up, towards God.

But then, did I still really trust God? I sensed immediately that a great deal depended upon my answer to this question. It had not been too difficult to trust him before. I had done so when, as a teenager, I had put my whole life into his hands.

That had been a magnificent, joyous moment of trust! A vital turning point. And I had slowly learned to trust him – often the hard way – through all the ups and downs which followed, discovering that trust was also a whole new way of life. True Christianity was trust! And out of this had grown the close relationship with Jesus which had become all-important to me. But what about now? Could I still trust him in these circumstances? I wasn't so sure.

A turmoil of 'whys?' had originally triggered this uncertainty. Why had God let this happen to me, just when I was so full of joyous confidence? Why did he allow far worse forms of suffering to happen to other people? Why? Why? Why? The questioning began to rub an uncomfortable groove across my mind. Now I found myself looking questioningly at God, rather than at the problem which had forced me into this close scrutiny of him. Was he still trustworthy? This was the key question.

I needed to be honest, open to seeing the entire situation in a different way, so that it confirmed rather than undermined my sense of God's trustworthiness. That was hard. I was so sure I had a legitimate grudge and that God must be brought to acknowledge this. (How little I really know of him!) In my bewilderment I admitted to God that suffering was an enigma to me and that, if I needed to see the whole matter from a new angle, then he'd have to give me both the will and the ability to do so.

I found myself starting to consider God. Had I ever before had reason to doubt his trustworthiness? No. Why? Because, being God, he was utterly good. That was part of what made him God. He was incapable of doing wrong, or of making mistakes. He could not even be tempted to do so. I knew that I had no alternative but to affirm God's complete trustworthiness, for no one had ever been able to present valid contrary evidence. And so, as a first step up out of my despair, I recognized that despite my barrage of 'whys' my basic understanding of God had not altered. He was still good! Had I not proved this over and over again in my own relationship with him? I affirmed all this quietly to myself that night, even though I was still distressed. It gave me something immediate to cling to. But I couldn't go any further. My mind was too tired.

It was over the next few days that this personal certainty of God's goodness gradually led me to see how such a confidence would satisfy my tangle of 'whys'. One morning I opened my Bible and read through the Book of Job wondering how he had sorted out all his desperate questioning. After all, Job had been through the most appalling suffering. Few others can have lost their possessions, all their children, and their health in such rapid succession. No wonder Job was completely torn apart. 'Why God, why? I don't deserve all this!' he cried. My own protests echoed his.

I realized, as I read further, that God understood Job's questioning. His empathy reached deeper than anyone else's ever could. God wasn't shocked or affronted by Job's 'why?'. Nor was he put on the spot. For all the intensity of the storm, God still had Job's affairs completely in hand. Nothing was out of control. God did not, however, answer Job's 'why'. (I recognized that he might not answer mine.) Instead he did something more difficult and more wonderful than offering explanations. He satisfied Job's questioning in a unique and completely effective way. God used the storm – the 'storm' of Job's grief, and a literal storm which moved steadily in towards Job's desolate home - as a backcloth for a tremendous drama:

'Then out of the storm God spoke to Job' (Job 38:1), God showed Job all the magnificence of his creation and answered him in a series of vivid picture-questions:

'Have you ever visited the storerooms where I keep the snow and the hail?' (38:22).

'Can you guide the stars season by season and direct the Great and Little Bear?' (38:32).

'Does an eagle wait for your command to build its nest high in the mountains?' (39:27).

'Can you catch Leviathan (a crocodile) with a fish-hook or tie his tongue down with a rope?' (41:1).

'Are you as strong as I am? Can your voice thunder as loud as mine?' (40:9).

I noticed that as God spoke, using word-picture after word-picture to illustrate his greatness and utter trustworthiness, Job was humbled into wondering silence. When at last he did find words there was no 'why' left. He said simply:

'I know, Lord, that you are all-powerful. You ask how I dare question your wisdom when I am so very ignorant. I talked about things I do not understand .... So I am ashamed of all I have said and repent' (42:2-6).

Job had seen God's magnificence, witnessed his all-controlling power. He didn't continue to insist on an answer for his 'why'. He didn't need one any longer. It was enough for him to know, beyond all doubt, that God was utterly good; that he was in control and completely worthy of trust. Job realized that if God cared so comprehensively for every lesser area of his creation, he cared even more for the people he had made. Nor could his care be brought into question by even the most violent sorrowing storm. The anguish merely served to make God's caring more immediate and vital. More tender. And I think that Job must have sensed that, even though he had lost his children, they were still safe – safer than before – in the care of God.

Still surrounded by his grief, Job worshipped God, even as in a very inadequate way I had worshipped that morning when I gazed on my baby. It is in such moments that trust is made strong, and all bitterness is finally overcome. I can see now that people often demand an answer for their 'whys' before they will offer God their full, unquestioning trust. 'Answer me, God, and then I will trust you!' they say. But that is entirely the wrong way round.

'Any satisfaction for our questioning is impossible until, like Job, we have first come to know God in a humbling, transforming way. Then out of this personal dependence can come confidence and we can truly say, 'He is trustworthy! This new oneness with him through love has proved it to me beyond all doubt!' And out of such confidence can come a calm acceptance. It is the essential sequence. We cannot find true satisfaction until we are first at one with the God from whom alone such satisfaction is derived.

'Satisfaction' is a key word. It may seem strange, but it is possible to be satisfied and at peace without needing to have an answer for every 'why'. (Our limited human minds would probably

not be able to grasp most of the answers anyway.)
Trust makes this possible. If we know that the God
to whom we've committed our whole lives is good,
and that even the most devastating experience is
still within his control, then it is possible to rest,
satisfied. Such an experience can even be turned
into value for us. Quite a few grieving and suffering people have spoken of the unexpected treas-
ure to be 'mined' out of a hard experience, as ex-
amples in this book show. Here is a safe, strong
place.

*Mysteries remain, but to those who hold the
Faith ... they are now mysteries of light and not
of darkness* (Sir Thomas Taylor).

Such a resting eventually made it possible for
me to recognize the first strands of daylight beyond the sorrowing storm. But it wasn't a sudden
transition from darkness to light. Moments, hours
and even days of distress still overwhelmed me at
times, just when I thought I was getting on top at
last. Even a small incident could trigger off an un-
reasonable amount of sorrow. I remember how a
snatch of poignant music would reduce me to tears
within seconds – music which, on previous occasions, brought immediate delight. It was bewildering to be so much at the mercy of unpredictable
emotions. As someone else has put it, speaking

after her husband's sudden death, 'There was no logic in it. I wasn't in control. I was a package of raw emotions tied together with loose string that had just come unravelled' (Elizabeth Mooney).

On such occasions I tried to check my tears, apologizing for them in embarrassment. But a friend stopped me. 'Tears are a safety valve,' she said. 'They'll bring you relief.' She was right. In the aloneness of those long night hours I would weep freely, sensing that I must cry if I was ever to know a healing of my sorrow. Then after a month or so, the weeping slowly lessened. I realized that I had moved a first step on beyond the sorrowing storm when I could listen to evocative music again – even to a friend's baby crying – without feeling the sudden prick of tears.

Something else began to be very important to me too. It was hope. As I held tightly to God with one hand I found myself more able to reach out towards the future with the other. Very slowly at first, just as far as 'tomorrow' or 'next week', and then in time to 'next month'. God was helping me to see that, for all the trauma of the storm, there was still a plan and a purpose ahead. There was still much more into which he was waiting to take me. But I had to see it through new eyes, allowing myself to be open to hopefulness and joy once more. That was hard. Self-pity and a longing for sympathy so often tried to drag me back, shutting off future possibilities. A grieving person once said that 'hope is always more important than happiness' (Katie F. Wiebe) and I slowly realized that this was true. Hope became possible to me even before I could imagine being happy again. It was the first shaft of strong, bright sunlight after the storm.

I was beginning to adjust. Looking back, I can see that various practical factors, as well as trust and hope, also helped to make that adjustment possible. One was solitude. Although family and friends played an important part in consoling me, solitude offered its own significant contribution too. I think that was why I instinctively sought the aloneness of those night hours during the early weeks of my sorrow. I was able to release my feelings in a way which wasn't possible when others, even my husband, were around. It wouldn't have been wise to prolong the solitude (at most it would last for a couple of hours each night) but I needed that time. It was valuable.

Valuable too was the need to accept practical help. Friends wanted to express their concern and this was one way in which they felt most able to show their caring for us. To offer to do something was easier than struggling for appropriate words to say. Most went straight ahead and collected a supermarket shopping list from me, filled cake tins, took the children out for a visit to the local zoo or asked us round for Sunday lunch. Few said, 'Let me know if there's anything I can do to help!' I wouldn't have known how to take them up on such an offer anyway. My mind wasn't functioning in a careful, ordered way. I wasn't able to work out what to ask each person to do. They had to think up such details for me, and most did.

My husband was the greatest help of all, offering support in numerous practical ways, but also in the deeper areas which no one else could share. The loss had been his too. He knew the pain of parental grief. Our relationship deepened through that shared experience and I recognized that deepening as an unexpected richness I was beginning to discover on the other side of loss.

It was also interesting to realize that the very ordinariness of happenings all around helped re-adjustment. At first I resented the fact that life in the busy, bustling city was the same as ever. Lorries still roared past up the nearby hill, taxis hooted impatiently at the slightest hold-up, street boys yelled out to each passer-by and donkey's hooves clattered on the uneven paving stones. Other mothers were cooking, cleaning, shopping, child minding around me.

Life was moving on just as usual, and I had to get busy with my own responsibilities too. I was needed. My husband and children were waiting for me to slip back into the role which only I could fulfil. And as far as possible I needed to be the same person, despite what had happened. Inside myself I wanted to forget about my appearance (what did it matter if I wore my housecoat all day and let my hair hang limp around my shoulders?) and forget about food too. (Wouldn't a quick sandwich now and then be enough?) But that would only allow grief to tighten instead of loose its hold. Those first valuable shafts of hope would fade and I would start to go back rather than forward. It was important to make myself dress neatly, set my hair, eat with the family and pick up the different threads which had been so suddenly dropped. It took time, it was often hard, but looking back I could say, 'It was good that I made myself be normal, if only for the family's sake.'

Normal? I sometimes wondered if normality was ever going to be possible again, and that question probably goes through every sorrowing person's mind. If normality means, 'everything being as it always was' then the answer is obviously 'No'. But then I discovered that the real meaning of the word is 'a usual pattern' and that seemed more possible. A goal to aim at. I felt that, given time, I could return to some sort of usual pattern. And now, looking back, I realize that doing so was vital. The alternative would have been to let a wretched sequence of regrets and memories play over and over through my mind, constantly laying open the wound of sorrow. As Katie F. Wiebe, a young widow, wrote:

'To live only with memories is to enter a prison of our own making and shut the door on the future.'

I have gone on much further into the future now and, from here, I can look on that experience of sorrow, tracing its unexpected value. I can for one thing, now understand how other mothers feel. I never knew before. When a neighbour here went through a similar experience recently I was able to empathize, rather than sympathize. It was a significant difference, offering us a much deeper bond with one another. Then too, I have sometimes been able to share words which were of particular comfort to me at the time when I was most desperate. They were written inside a card sent by an older, single lady:

One day you will have him to hold in heaven.

What a refuge that truth offered to me! It was as if strong arms of comfort had been suddenly thrown right around me, and the relief was immediate. I *would* see and delight in my child again! I would know him to be mine, and for ever too! That realization proved to be a turning point, filling me with far-reaching future hope.

I can see how the fulfilment of this hope will one day illustrate for me the fact of God's complete goodness and trustworthiness. For in heaven our trust will turn into seeing, and our seeing into the delight of full experience. And then how magnificent to our new eyes God's goodness will be! We'll wonder how we could ever have doubted him!

Chapter Four

The loss of a child

**'Dawn knew she was dying . . .
yet she was happy.'**

If a mother is mourning not for what she herself has lost but for what her dead child has lost, it is a comfort to believe that the child has not lost the end for which it was created. And it is a comfort to believe that she herself, in losing her chief or only happiness, has not lost a greater thing, that she may still hope to 'glorify God and enjoy him forever.' A comfort to the God-aimed eternal spirit within her. (C. S. Lewis, *A Grief Observed*)

Of a young girl: 'She had so much to live for. I thought, though more to die for.' (Gladys Hunt)

In that day . . . a little child shall lead them all (Isaiah 11:6 TLB).

The deep snow is lingering. (I still yearn for Ethiopia's warmth and colourfulness!) The roads around our home are covered with a thick, hazardous crust of ice. What a loud crunching noise every time a car passes our house! I haven't been able to enjoy cycle rides to the village for weeks, but walking offers its own interest and pleasure too. I decided to take the footpath up beside the primary school this morning. It's a quick route to the corner shop. The mid-morning break was in full swing. Excited shrieks and shouts were echoing across the wide, white playing field, the loudest shouts of all coming from the far end where a small slope was covered in thick ice. I could see older lads trying to keep their balance as they jostled each other down the shining slide. A cluster of smaller boys and girls were gazing in admiration, sometimes clapping their cold hands in delight.

The path took me up past the swings and I noticed a carpet of thick, rough ice spread beneath their lopsided seats. Five small boys were stamping the ice into sharp fragments, giggling with satisfaction as it shattered beneath their boots. There were children all up the path. Some using scarves as tow ropes to tug friends along, some standing silent and shivering, some picking at potato crisps with their stiff fingers, some trying to release an ice-bound Cola can from a nearby puddle, some skidding after an old punctured ball. Five-year-old

Catriona crept shyly up to me, smiling from beneath her furry hood, unsure of what to say.

'Hullo there! How are you today?' I began.

'Nae bad!' And she skipped away back to her friends.

The bell rang. Loud and shrill and unwelcome. Before the last shriek had died away there was a sudden swoop of gulls and crows – they had been waiting along the roof edges of nearby houses anticipating this moment – and fierce squabbling began. I watched as each abandoned crisp packet was pounced upon and fought over, amid a scattering of salty crumbs. And the angry black-headed gulls could still be heard even when I was far up the path, almost within sight of the shop.

The picture of those children, the picture of young Catriona coming to meet me, is still vivid in my mind. I realize what particular pleasure small children give now that my own three have grown beyond primary-school age. Catriona has helped to recapture those earlier days for me, making memories live again. I hope I shall never forget what I have learned through watching and listening to a small child. Children have so much to share! They long for us to stop still, to understand, even sometimes to become as a little child again.

This need to stop still and to understand recently became very important to a young mother in our area here. Her daughter was seriously ill and in need of constant care, yet in those last months and weeks together the little girl so clearly shared her simple, strong faith in Jesus Christ that the mother was able to see dying and bereavement in a new, completely different way.

I will let this mother tell her own experience, just as she described it to me one morning recently when we were sitting together around the fireside in her small city flat. (Eileen's three-year-old son, Ian, was there too, sipping at a cup of milk and scribbling his way through a thick pile of notepaper.)

'Our little girl, Dawn, was nine when she died,' Eileen told me. 'That was two years ago now. Two years tomorrow.'

She paused to pick up the biscuit crumbs Ian had dropped.

'Was she ill for very long?' I asked.

'Two years. I guessed almost immediately that something serious was wrong. I remember it so clearly. It was a dark February afternoon and Dawn hadn't come in from school. 'What's happened to her?' my husband said. We were worried, so I went out into the street and there she was, just dragging herself towards home. Very slowly, her heavy school bag weighing her down.

'As soon as I reached her I noticed the dark rings under her eyes. 'Maybe she's got the measles,' I thought. It was going round, like it does in winter.

I suddenly remembered that she'd had a faint rash
the night before when I bathed her. Anyway, I took
Dawn to the doctor that night and he thought it
might be measles. He also did a blood test.

'Next morning the doorbell rang. It was the doctor. "Take Dawn down to the children's hospital
straight away," he said. "Go this morning. They're
expecting her."

'I think that was when I realized Dawn might
be seriously ill. I didn't want to believe it, yet the
fear kept forcing its way into my mind. I phoned
my mother and I hardly knew what to say. I was
shaking all over as I stood in the phone box.

'Of course, as soon as Dawn reached the hospital – it's just down the road from here – they
admitted her and began all the tests. They had to
take her to the theatre for one of them, and the
doctors let me stay with her. It helped Dawn to
have me there holding her hand, but tests like that
are a hard experience for a mother. You just sit there
watching, with a big lump in your throat. You don't
cry, not until you get home . . .'

Eileen paused. Tears filled her blue eyes, but I
knew she wanted to go on.

'Soon afterwards they told me the news. My
husband was there as well as the three doctors. I
knew it was coming. Dawn had got leukaemia.
"How long will it be?" I asked them. They didn't
know. "Maybe two years,' they said. Those few

minutes in the doctor's room kept going over and over in my mind. I'd heard the words they'd said but I couldn't take it all in. The treatment began straight away. One evening they told me "All Dawn's hair will have to be cut off," and then the ward sister drew the curtains round her bed and began. She had the most beautiful hair. It hung down in thick ringlets – all natural – and was so long she could sit on it.

'I stayed with Dawn for a long time that evening, trying to cheer her up. The other children were asleep so they hadn't seen what had happened. Then I ran out into the grounds round the hospital and began to scream. That was the turning point for me, I suddenly realized the truth of what was happening to Dawn. It all became real.

'Next morning I went to the ward early and found they'd given Dawn a short ginger wig. She looked awful. Her face was pale and puffed out because of the drugs she was on. The wig didn't look right at all. I wanted to scream, "What have you done to my baby?" but I knew I mustn't let Dawn see how I felt. That same day I went to the shops and chose a pretty wig which suited her much better.'

Eileen stopped to pour me a second cup of tea. 'Do you think every parent has to reach a turning point of some kind?' I asked.

'Yes!' Eileen insisted. 'Yes, it's very important.

After that, you can begin to accept what's happening. Sometimes when friends hear the news they say, "Don't worry. It'll be all right. Doctors can do such marvellous things nowadays." But that's not helpful. It's a way of covering up the truth and then, in the end, everything becomes so much harder. If you can bring yourself to accept what is happening right from the start then you can cope better. You begin to pack as much as possible into those last years. That's what I did after that night. I knew I must make the most of Dawn while I still had her.

'Mind you, I didn't spoil her. I still "raged" her when she was making trouble. Of course I did. Life had to be as normal as possible. Most of the mothers in the ward said the same thing about "accepting" and then enjoying the time still left with their children. We could understand each other's thoughts about it. But one mother kept herself to herself. She didn't go along with the way we felt. We tried to include her, but she just couldn't see it our way. She kept on fighting what was happening to her child and it meant that she was a very sad person. Lonely too. We just couldn't get through to her.'

'Did you ever hold out hope that Dawn would get better?'

'No, never. Maybe that sounds strange, but I didn't. Of course, much as I wanted her to get bet-

ter, I was afraid it wouldn't last. Then she'd have
to suffer all over again. I didn't want that for her.
So when I prayed for Dawn I just asked that she
wouldn't have to go through a lot of suffering. That
was all. My husband's parents felt differently. They
prayed for Dawn to be completely healed. I was
grateful to them, but I didn't feel able to pray like
that. I just put Dawn in God's hands.'

Eileen was silent for a few moments, and I could
tell that her mind was going back over the years.
She was seeing Dawn again, visualizing her daughter, and the fun they'd shared together, even in those
last months.

'I remember Dawn's seventh birthday,' Eileen
said suddenly. 'She was just out of hospital and
we made a real celebration of it. Then later that
summer we all went to a very remote part of Scotland – way over on the west coast – and spent a
couple of weeks in a hired caravan. It was beautiful there! Just one cottage nearby, and then the river
and mountains. Oh, and the horses too. Dawn was
a fantastic rider, so she just loved it all. And we let
her ride as much as she wanted. I remember that
she took off her wig while we were on holiday.

'The fresh air will make my hair grow again!'
she told us. And maybe she was right because by
the time school began again her own hair was just
long enough to be nicely styled. Not that any of
her friends would have teased her. Everyone at the

school was full of concern for Dawn. They were very kind.

'She was determined to work hard and keep up with her classes, so the different teachers encouraged her and brought work here to the house if she had to miss a few days of school. Dawn just worked and worked. She loved it. Her lessons meant a lot to her. She studied all kinds of extra things too, like ancient Egyptian history and art. Even when she was in hospital she'd be writing in her school book with one hand while the drip needle was stuck into the other.

'And she kept up with activities at the church, and at Brownies too. She was determined to get as many badges as she could. About the last thing she did was to go swimming with her friends, just a day or two before they took her back into hospital.'

The fire was burning low. Eileen fetched some more coal. 'I'll never forget those last weeks,' she said quietly. 'One day Dawn put her school books down and never looked at them again. She just stopped working. She knew. I stayed with Dawn as much as possible. The ward sister was a very caring person, very devoted. She let me come and go any time. It was like that for all the parents. And the social worker was a marvellous person, just like a mother hen. She took me under her wing and cared for me. We're still very close. She'd support me whenever it was extra hard, but I managed to go through it all.

'I'm quite a strong person and can take a lot. The worst part of all was seeing Dawn suffer and not being able to relieve her pain as I'd almost always been able to do before – with small cuts and bruises, and so on. Now it was different, and it was very, very hard. But I was *with* her, holding her hand and sharing it. That made a tremendous difference. She was never alone, at least not when she was awake. In Dawn's case the terminal stage was very, very bad. It isn't always like that, but it was for her. I needed to stay close to my little girl all the time, even though it hurt me to see her like that. Right at the end it was peaceful though. Very peaceful – an answer to my prayers. I was peaceful too. I felt the caring of everyone around us. All the staff, our minister and church friends. It really comforted me.

'That last evening Dawn seemed to be asleep, but she suddenly opened her eyes and said, "I'm not coming back down again, and I *don't* want corned beef and chips for my tea!" We couldn't help smiling. She'd said it so clearly and calmly. I think she knew what was happening. At eight o'clock she asked me to turn the electric fan off. And then at five past she died. It was as quiet as that. Peaceful. I didn't want the stillness to be broken, so I stayed sitting by the bed for about ten

minutes, holding Dawn's hand. I didn't call anyone, I didn't ring the bell. I just wanted that time
to be alone with my little girl ...

'Of course, I had to go home eventually, but I
did see Dawn again. They brought her to the flat
two days later and when I looked down at her she
was absolutely beautiful. Just like a doll. A new
person! All I could feel was relief. That is how I
remember her now. She looked so beautiful ...'

The room was silent for a few seconds, except
for young Ian wriggling beside me and turning the
pages of a picture book.

'You know,' Eileen said suddenly, 'Dawn really
knew Jesus Christ. She knew he died for her and
because of this she really loved him. She'd given
her whole self to him. The story of the cross meant
a lot to her, right from the first time she heard it.
When Dawn was only seven she drew a picture of
Jesus dying on the cross. Our minister was so taken
with it that he had it framed and hung on the ves-
tibule wall of our church. It's still there. Dawn was
interested in the Bible too and she read it a lot. I
think this helped her when she was dying because
she knew where she was going. Dawn had a very
strong, very simple faith in Jesus and so she knew
she'd go to be there in heaven with him.

'All along she'd accepted dying, and she was
quite calm and happy about it. Some people might
not believe that, but it's true. Dawn even chose her

funeral hymn. I found it marked in her hymn book the day after she died. I opened her school bag and there it was:

> *If I come to Jesus*
> *He will hear my prayers;*
> *He will love me dearly;*
> *He my sins did bear.*
> *If I come to Jesus,*
> *He will take my hand,*
> *He will kindly lead me*
> *To a better land.*

'I think all of us at the funeral were very moved as we sang those words. It was as if Dawn was right there with us.'

Eileen fetched the hymn book to show me Dawn's hymn. 'We were very close, Dawn and I,' she said slowly. 'When she first took ill I thought I was being punished. But I wasn't. I know that now. God didn't put diseases into the world. He's not responsible for them. In fact, Jesus was sent here to heal illness. But everyone puts the blame onto him. If only they'd believe instead of blaming him, then they'd be able to find comfort for their sorrow. Even the worst pain and sorrow is comforted. I know that, because I've received so much comfort for my own sorrow.

'At first I kept on asking 'Why me?' but then I

realized that suffering and sorrow happen to everyone. All kinds of people. Some are worse off
than me – like my friend who lost a husband and
two children. I've never ever been bitter about what
happened to Dawn. I think that's because, as I
watched her simple trust in Jesus, my own faith
became much stronger. If I hadn't had that faith I
don't know how I would have carried on. A personal faith in God really does mean everything ...'

I knew I must go. It was getting near to lunch
time and Ian would be hungry. But there was still
one question left in my mind. It had come to me as
a result of hearing another bereaved parent say,
'Our two-year-old daughter's life was short yet it
was a life fully lived.' *Fully* lived, even though the
little girl died when she was only a toddler? Had
that life been fully lived? Had Dawn's?

'Yes, I do feel that Dawn's live was fully lived.'
Eileen insisted. 'It was complete. Nothing important was left undone.' She paused, smiling. 'See
that tapestry on the shelf? The picture of a country
cottage? Dawn made that for me only a few weeks
before she died. I knew she wasn't feeling at all
well and so tried to get her to stop sewing and rest.
But she wouldn't

' "I'm going to finish it for you, Mummy!" she
kept saying. And she did. She completed every single stitch. I went out and bought a frame straight
away, and Dawn was thrilled when she saw me hang

her picture up. It was like a parable. Her life was ending, yet she lived it fully until the here-and-now part of it was all complete.'

I thought about Dawn's tapestry as I drove slowly back along the snowy Aberdeenshire lanes towards our home. I could see what her mother meant and I began to recognize that from God's point of view every life is lived until it is complete. With him there are no sudden interruptions, no unexpected, unplanned endings. Each life is a whole. I could see, too, that Dawn's tapestry was a parable of how that small girl saw her own brief life. Nothing important was missing. And because it was a complete life she was able to come to terms with what was happening. She was able to accept dying, even to feel happy at the thought of Jesus – whom she knew so closely – 'kindly leading her to a better land.'

It was also true that Dawn's acceptance had made all the difference to her mother's exacting experience. She had learnt to watch and listen to her small daughter, becoming almost 'as a little child' again in her own growing faith and confidence. This was to prove vital to her in the days which followed Dawn's funeral. Inevitably the anguish of bereavement was very intense, yet she still clung to God. Jesus Christ had become as dear to her as he was to Dawn. In a very real sense they were still together, in him, and always would be.

Eileen's parting words that morning have lingered in my mind. 'I think I called Dawn the right name,' she smiled, as we stood together at the door. 'Because her life here was only the beginning of so much more!'

Chapter Five

Illness and death

**'We've been learning about death
through learning about life!'**

There is a sadness growing
Within me
I do not want it so, but
I know
I cry with bitterness
Filling me.
It does not hurt the way
It did
Yesterday.

There is only room for
Just so much sorrow.
What will I put in
Its place
Tomorrow?

(Written by Beth, a forty-two-year-old patient who knew she was dying, and taken from Elizabeth Kubler-Ross and Mal Warsham, *To Live Until We say Goodbye*)

Death is but the beginning of something far greater. Dying makes life suddenly real. Watching my slow physical deterioration reaffirmed my belief that there is something else within, which would survive. (Dr. James Casson, *Dying, the Greatest Adventure of my Life*)

Resting in the hope of eternal life, life which the ever truthful God who cannot deceive, promised before the world or the ages of time began (Titus 1:2 Amp.).

Twice this week a small flock of whooper swans has passed overhead. They are amongst our winter visitors from the Arctic. It seems impossible that they could have travelled such a distance. Their flight looks so slow and laboured, and the more so against fierce winds. Yet each arrowed formation is a marvellous sight, compelling me to stop and gaze in admiration as the group beats steadily on across the empty sky.

Sometimes the sun shines all through the brief day, touching the slopes of Bennachie with a first red flush around 9 am and then rising strong and golden to light up the wide, white world. Every tree and bush and insignificant grass blade is encased in sparkling ice. Cobwebs are draped like starched lace on the fence wire by the river.

We have never seen such a deep fall of snow before (nearly two feet on the lawn this morning) nor felt the cold bite so fiercely at our ears and noses. When walking to the village shops I have to blink often in order to keep my eyelashes from freezing together. The children are recording each day's temperatures – sometimes as low as -21 degrees C – and on the most bitter mornings the cold rushes in like white smoke as soon as we open the back door.

The Don is almost blocked by ice; just one narrow channel is still running. The swift-flowing water makes a loud sucking noise as it licks far beneath the ice flats. All the birds look dejected, particularly the crows. Tired and silent, they linger in the topmost branches of the beeches while far below blackbirds hop from hawthorn to hawthorn, scattering ice dust as they go.

Everywhere there is a strange desolation, an awesome stillness. As winter approached we thought we were familiar with its moods, well able to cope with every demand. But now it has overwhelmed us again. And it goes on and on, tightening its icy grip as the days drag past. Will the thick white crust ever melt? Is there still green grass beneath? Will the skylark soon sing again, and frail snowdrops crowd the riverside woods? Will spring ever come?

Hope! How often I find myself clinging to it through this long, dark winter. Friends in the village tell us that it is one of the coldest winters in living memory. One of the longest too. 'And there'll aye be worse to come this month!' an older gentleman informed me yesterday as we stood together in the post-office queue.

But surely it won't last much beyond March? There is spring to anticipate! Already I find myself thinking ahead to those first joyous hints of its coming – a gleaming crocus opening up to the pale sun, the glad returning shrieks of oyster-catchers bustling in across the sky, the flash of a dipper skimming low above the Don with nesting grass

in its beak. Each offers a foretaste of spring, full
of significance and delight – and greatly strength-
ening my hope.

Hope has an important part to play in so many
other aspects of our lives too. We are made for
hope; our lives are constantly geared to it. We hope
for simple everyday happenings – the visit of a
friend, the arrival of a letter – and we hope for
long-term goals such as the gaining of a qualifica-
tion or being promoted at work. Hope fills our
thoughts, offering incentive and overriding hard
work or temporary setbacks. It maintains our confidence even when everything seems to be stacked
against us. Hope is strong inward power, compelling us to reach out towards the future.

And yet how difficult it must be for the people
facing a life-threatening illness to retain those
hopes which have hitherto been so important to
them. Even the word 'hope' seems to mock them
in their suffering. It is a bewildering position to be
in. On the one hand a person fears that he now has
no valid reason for hopefulness, while on the other
he still craves for even one firm goal towards which
he can move. Throughout his life he has been mo-
tivated by all kinds of different hopes. Is there nothing to hope for now?

'Yes, there is!' a hospital social worker insisted
when talking to a group of us in the village last
week. 'And hope is vital to our patients. Perhaps

more important to them now than it has ever been before.'

As this skilled counsellor explained different aspects of her work to us, I noticed that 'hope' was mentioned over and over again, despite the fact that her ministry centred around people suffering from cancer.

'One of our main aims is to give a patient different reasons for hopefulness,' she told us. 'Practical workable reasons too. Realistic goals towards which they can work. These have to be introduced at the right time, of course. Initially the diagnosis triggers overwhelming shock and disbelief, particularly if a person is young and feeling quite healthy. "It just can't have happened to me!" he will say over and over again, and for the time being he cannot concentrate on anything other than the impossible aspect of it all.

'Eventually, as the truth sinks in, a patient is likely to become angry and resentful. The whole thing seems so devastating, so unfair. He may try to persuade himself that he would rather never have known, and yet at the same time he senses that the truth is far better than deception. Every patient in our department is aware of his diagnosis. That is our consultant's policy and it's wise. It provides us with a clear basis of openness and trust from which we can begin to work together. There are times, however, when the *full* truth is withheld because a patient isn't able to take it all in at that initial stage. But nevertheless they are given the score and enough detail to help them cope with the next few steps ahead. Before long, patients realize that our whole team is right behind them, offering skilled support and treatment, and this begins to ease their distress and fear.

'My first priority is to sit and listen as a patient shares his very normal reactions to disbelief and anger. It is important for him to express these deep feelings. In time a relationship of trust grows up between us, and then different members of the medical team are able to suggest goals towards which the patient can begin to move. Goals which will rekindle hope and so help to overcome anger and resentment. These may be such things as starting on a specific course of treatment, then completing it and being able to go home. There will also be talk of 'When you can start back at work' or 'When you can resume your training.' These different, quite valid hopes make all the difference for our patients, giving them incentive to go on. Without hope they can so quickly sink into despair. Then, of course, it's also important to remember that rapid advances in the treatment of malignant disease are offering patients increasing long-term hope. Recovery *is* possible for some.'

As I sat listening to the social worker I couldn't help thinking of my nephew, Simon. Dark-haired, with an eager smiling face, he is just sixteen and has been suffering from an unusual form of leukaemia for the past two and a half years. If any youngster could have had reason to be full of happy anticipation about a future career it was this lad. Long before his illness was discovered he had shown above-average ability at school and was keen to train as a doctor eventually.

'Simon soaks up all the medical information he can lay his hands on!' my sister, Wendy, once commented and, being a nurse herself, she encouraged her son's interest in medicine. In one medical magazine Simon came across a lengthy article about leukaemia and read it in detail. Then, soon afterwards his own illness was diagnosed and inevitably his first reaction was, 'I think I know what I've got. Is it leukaemia?'

Since then he has undergone lengthy courses of drug treatment, but despite expert medical care, there have been many serious reverses in Simon's condition. More than once an encouraging remission has been brought to a sudden end by the return of ominous symptoms. Just when Simon has felt more able to cope with the exacting demands of his illness it has overwhelmed him again, almost without warning. 'We live each day and week as it comes now,' Wendy said recently. 'It's less traumatic that way.'

But despite this, Simon is careful to maintain

his goals. Hopes and ideas continue to be significant and important to him. This was obvious recently when he spoke to me about his illness in a frank and straightforward way. I will share all he said so that the reality of his different hopes and plans will be seen within the wider setting of his difficult circumstances:

'I've always known the score, right from the start. Ignorance wouldn't have been bliss at all. I needed to know. Of course, when I first discovered what was wrong with me I thought, "I'll be completely better in a few months' time", not realizing that it would be such a long fight and that the drugs have to be taken for at least five years before you can be really hopeful about a cure. I didn't know anything about that. Nor did I know all the details about the different treatments used at the Unit I attend. It's better not to know *everything*! Looking back, I'm glad I wasn't fully aware of what was in store for me.

'When people visit me I notice that they're afraid to ask directly about my illness. They're always so tactful, picking words with such care. It's very annoying. I like people to be more direct and open, so I try to put them at ease. It's important for them to know that I'm not always in pain and feeling sick. Most of the time I feel normal. One hundred per cent! I've told my teenage friends everything, so they know the score, and now they tend to leave the subject alone. I think they're afraid to upset me by asking direct questions, although they have asked me in the past and I've answered them – so it may be that they don't have any questions left.

'When I'm feeling unwell I like to just lie on the sofa and sleep, or watch TV, or think about what I'm going to do when I feel better. Having short-term plans and ideas is very important to me. It helps a lot. Gives me something to look forward to. All through my illness I've made plans about things I'd like to do when I'm back in action again. Deep-sea fishing trips, visits to friends, and so on. Of course, I *have* missed out on things the rest of the family have been able to do. My brother Pete sometimes goes fishing without me. Or maybe I'm in hospital having a transfusion and can't join him and Louise (my sister) when they go off socializing with our friends. The two of them went on that holiday abroad too, and I had to miss it. I've often wished I could share in all these things. I've just found that ... well ... very sad.

'But I *did* get out to see Dad in Kenya last Easter. That was very nice. It was only a pity that Louise and Pete couldn't be with us too.

'I've missed a lot of school but I hope it won't affect my chances too much. I've just taken my O' level selection tests in biology, and I'll be sitting the physics in a couple of weeks' time. The biology should be all right. I'm hopeful about it. Of course the actual O-levels aren't for a few months yet so I've got time.

'On the 'gains' side of being ill I've enjoyed a lot more attention from Mum! I'm definitely much more spoilt than I used to be. And it's nice not to have to do energetic things like gardening. Sometimes I get out of the washing-up too.

'Since we started the Fund to raise money for bone-marrow transplants all kinds of exciting things have happened to me. There's been lots of publicity about it and I find this quite enjoyable – sometimes. There have been several sponsored events and this afternoon I've just come back from watching a local Walk. Having this Fund to plan and think about has helped me a great deal. We're always getting new ideas for it. I like thinking ahead, whether it's for the Fund, or for my own career. I must admit that I sometimes feel a menacing twinge at the back of my mind as to whether I'll be here in the next decade. But I try to dismiss it and tell myself not to be so stupid. "You'll be cured!" I'm not entirely frightened of death itself, just the thought of not being able to be with the family. The thought of everything going on as it always used to, and me not having a part in the goings-on . . .

'My faith in God has helped tremendously in this illness. I can't think what non-believers do

when they get ill. My faith has been strengthened
a lot. Before I got ill I always thought of myself as
a Christian because I went to church and did all
the usual things. Sometimes anyway! But now I
really appreciate the whole concept of Christianity. It's much more than just going to Sunday services. It's really knowing God. Belonging to him
somehow. When I'm feeling ill I always pray and
it helps a lot.

'The fact that God is backing me up all the way
is a great morale-booster in this little battle, I find.
So are the postcards, letters and all sorts of things
that people send to cheer me up. Verses from the
Bible and parables help too. I'm very aware of the
powerful effect of prayer from the many people
who are praying for me. Mum and I have just been
talking about this. My own feeling is that the power
from their prayer is going up to God, and then coming from God to me. I know this because when
I'm unwell Mum and I still seem to be at ease in
knowing that everything is going to be OK.

'I definitely believe in a God of love despite
my illness, because it is all leading to something
really big in my life. I was angry at the beginning
when I didn't understand, and that same anger returned when my first relapse occurred. After going through two years of hard fighting, that big
setback was so depressing. But since then I've
deliberately said to myself, "God is in control.

Don't worry." This helps an enormous amount and now I'm beginning just to take things as they come. When I do relapse I try to put the facts behind me and get back into remission as soon as possible.'

Simon's words revealed an unusual courage and optimism, particularly those last few sentences. As he spoke I realized that he was illustrating for me what the social worker had already said. Hope is still possible for seriously ill patients; in fact it is essential if they are going to be able to cope with what has happened. I've recognized too that this hope is most valuable when it is focused first upon the immediate situation, then a step or two into the future and then a few steps more. In this way hope is made real and convincing to a suffering person, because it starts right where they are and points to a way ahead which, until then, they had not considered possible.

In her talk, the social worker showed how that first focus of hope becomes real when another person (close to the patient and trusted by him) enables him to see that, despite all, there are still different, helpful factors at work in his immediate circumstances: (1) he is in the hands of a skilled medical team who will be able to carefully assess his condition; (2) soon afterwards appropriate treatment will be started, bringing relief; and (3) longer-term possibilities will then eventually be explored.

All of these are important, relevant factors dur-

ing those early, desperate days when the truth of a
diagnosis can hardly be comprehended. They give
the patient something firm to hold onto despite
his fear and bewilderment. Simon was helped in
this way. Immediately after his diagnosis had been
made, he was stunned by the implications of so
serious and unusual an illness. He had only just
read up all the facts. They were in the forefront of
his mind. But then the consultant presented various proposals for treatment and Simon slowly began to hope again, to expect relief and the even-
tual onset of a remission. As he himself said later,
'When the doctor explained what he was going to
do I thought, "Now I can look forward to being
better!" '

Then, as treatment is started, a person can slowly
begin to feel his way ahead to the short-term future. This will be hard for a patient experiencing
unpleasant side-effects of drugs and radiation, but
even then the expectation of eventually being one
step further on can help him to keep going through
an otherwise very exacting period. Some of these
plans and ideas for the future appear simple and
basic – like having a haircut or perm, going out
for a ride in the car during visiting hours etc. – but
they are significant, for each represents definite
progress.

As these goals are reached, others will replace
them. A young mother who is ill in hospital may

ask if she will be home in time for her young son's birthday and, if that's a possibility, she will eagerly look forward to the date. If unexpected problems prevent her actually being with her family for the event her acute disappointment may be comforted by having the little boy visit her in hospital. An older man may look forward to being out of hospital in time to supervise the planting of his vegetable garden at home, or the start of a new project at work. A middle-aged mother may look forward to being home in time for the arrival of her first grandchild. All these are valuable goals towards which each step of hope can move.

Simon has his particular aims in view too: 'I'm studying hard for that physics selection test in two weeks' time!' 'It will be great to go deep-sea fishing with Pete next month!' He has also learnt that his hopes may not always be realized – the urgent need for a blood transfusion means cancellation of a weekend visit to friends, the sudden onset of a relapse rules out deep-sea fishing for a while – but after the initial pain of disappointment he slowly replaces his cancelled hopes with new ideas, and starts again. He has to. Over the long months since his illness began he has come to realize that, 'Even if I'm sometimes disappointed, short-term goals still help a lot. They give me important reasons for thinking and looking ahead. I need them!'

Simon's statement 'I need them!' might well

be echoed by many others in his position. But thinking ahead with hopefulness is far from easy in such circumstances. Sometimes it is intensely hard, requiring constant determination. There will inevitably be times (particularly at the onset of a relapse) when despair returns and future goals rapidly fade. 'Is it really worth struggling on?' Since Simon spoke with me he has been through several low and bewildering days, wanting only to lie down and withdraw from all that had previously occupied his eager mind and kept him going.

'When he's going through a rough patch we just let him have his own quiet corner of the sitting room, and fit in with what he wants to do,' Wendy explained recently. 'If Simon feels like eating I try to cook the food he particularly requests. If he doesn't want any meals I just give him drinks of milk or fruit juice. If he decides to join us on a short car outing then we help him to dress and he comes along. If he's too weak then maybe Louise or Pete will stay around while I go. Simon and I need a break from one another sometimes because inevitably, when life is suddenly so intense, there's a terrific build-up of pressure. A break eases it for a while. It's very important.'

After a few days Simon will gradually begin to think about his school selection tests again, or maybe an idea for the Fund comes into his mind. Then too, the postman often brings letters of response connected with this, and Simon likes to be able to read and consider them. Gradually he feels able to start looking ahead, and hope for the short-term future becomes possible once again.

It is interesting to note that in his case, this rekindling of hopefulness has not necessarily coincided with an improvement in his physical condition. Sometimes, when his blood count is at a disturbing level, he is full of eager ideas and plans. 'The doctors just don't know how he's managing to keep going at the moment. It's a mystery!' Wendy told me last week. With a laboratory report which indicated an exceptionally high presence of leukaemia cells, he was still up and about and cheerfully insisting on going to a school disco. 'I've just got to see my friends, Mum. I haven't had a chat with them for *ages*!'

As I've thought about Simon and many other patients in similar circumstances, I've remembered that although hope is essential to them, they still have to cope with the fact that they are suffering from a life-threatening illness. Hope can significantly alter their response to that fact, but the diagnosis remains. At times its reality can almost be forgotten, particularly during a period of steady improvement. But for those, like Simon, who experience frequent rough patches and setbacks there will be periods of acute sorrow and fear. Is there any future to anticipate and plan for?

Close relatives feel this anguish too. It is heart-rending to watch a young lad like Simon steadily changing from the strong energetic teenager he used to be only two or three years ago. It is hard to see him fighting weakness and frustration, while also sensing that the long battle against physical disease may eventually be lost. Nothing, not even his eager hopes, can completely cover such apprehension and sorrow, nor lessen the physical ordeal which he and many other patients experience. It would be wrong to so emphasize hope that the suffering aspect of such an illness was played down.

For some patients, too, there will come a time when it is no longer possible to look for a recovery, or even a lengthy remission. The illness has progressed too far. For all his eager hopefulness and forward planning, this is the stage which Simon has now reached. It is intensely hard both for him and his family. No one can fully understand unless they have known that experience too. A young doctor, Dr. James Casson, has spoken frankly about this overwhelming moment of realization. In a short booklet, *Dying, The Greatest Adventure of my Life,* written during the last weeks of his life, he described his reaction when a secondary growth of cancer was discovered:

I was in a cruel new world and I was on my own, or so it seemed. I was dying. I kept waking up in the night supposing I had been having a bad dream, but a quick feel in my armpit confirmed that the lump was there. I was trapped like an animal in a cage .... Never in my professional career had I realized what a burden this diagnosis, in particular, places on a person. The effect was total.

This is the moment at which, inevitably, everything changes. A person yearns for that which was safe and familiar. He longs for physical security, and yet he knows that this is now impossible. He has entered a 'cruel new world'; a world where all previous plans and ideas seem suddenly to have become irrelevant. They no longer matter. But what *does* matter? What can a person cling to now? Is there any kind of hope which still holds meaning?

At this stage (if not earlier on in the illness) a person may well decide to put his hope in various non-medical forms of healing, feeling compelled to 'try anything'. I found Dr. Casson's brief comments on 'Divine Healing' helpful, particularly his sharing of personal experience. He tells how his prayers for healing eventually took the form of a simple, clear-cut committal of his difficult situation into God's hands, and in this way he experienced the divine intervention for which he had been searching:

There was no doubt that 'healing' took place for me at an emotional level during a time when I was very depressed about my condition. Furthermore, there were specific answers to prayer about a number of most distressing symptoms. In particular I was relieved of nausea and vomiting . . . However, the conflict of whether 'I was doing everything correctly' did trouble me. Release came with the realization that the whole issue was out of my hands. One morning I had a clear picture that I was in a boat. Before, when asking for healing, it was as though I was in a punt where one stands at one end pushing on a punt pole and steering with more or less expertise. Afterwards, I was in a rowing boat, my back to the direction I was going, but travelling in a much more leisurely fashion. The great joy was that the Lord was at the tiller, his face gently smiling and his eyes twinkling as he guided me to my destination. Was I healed? Yes I believe I was.

Other people may be healed in an even more spectacular way. It's true, God does heal! And although it is not for us to specify the exact form such healing must take, there is certainly a very real place for deliberately committing the whole bewildering situation to God. An unexpected rest in the matter then becomes possible – like resting back in the rowing boat – and healing in one form or another will indeed be experienced, just as Dr. Casson discovered.

So many other things are discovered at this stage too. Dr. Casson indicated this when he said, *'Dying makes life suddenly real.'* Earlier on he had been much like anyone else, full of career goals and legitimate personal ambitions. He had enjoyed planning home improvements or summer holidays, and had also been glad to undertake his different responsibilities within the family or at work. He had had so many varying hopes and ideas, each absorbing at the time and demanding careful thought and consideration.

But now everything was changing. His very circumstances made work, holidays and most home responsibilities impossible. Together with many other considerations they began to fall behind in his list of priorities as he realized that, they were not of prime importance after all.

But life itself began to seem more and more precious:

'It was as if I suddenly started really to live, although the reverse was true and I was dying .... A clear spring morning is most meaningful after weeks of dull wet weather. So life can only really be understood when it is contrasted with death.'

This is the moment at which even the simplest

pleasures – the song of a solitary robin, the sight of a glistening cobweb, the laugh of a little child, the glow of a crimson sunset – are suddenly filled with new meaning and delight. Every moment begins to be savoured while it may yet be enjoyed. Life suddenly becomes vivid and compelling. A dying person longs to be allowed to do anything which will heighten that awareness and bring him joy.

It was for this reason that Simon's doctors recently encouraged Wendy to take him back to visit the country where he was born – Kenya. She had been wanting to do this (her husband works in East Africa) but was hesitant about possible risks. 'You go. It will mean a lot to Simon,' the specialist said, and so they went. And 'mean a lot' was an understatement!

Simon just revelled in it all: his grandparents' farm, the herds of familiar game which roamed in the grasslands and forests not far away, the smell of dust and the sound of heavy rain on a tin roof. Every rekindled memory was rich with enjoyment for them all, and the more so because Simon was allowed to enter as fully as possible into those different pleasures.

Perhaps life never seems so sweet as when we suddenly realize that it is drawing to a close.

There is a sadness growing
Within me
I do not want it so, but
I know . . .

With that 'knowing' of the truth, that poignant
realization of dying, comes a great yearning to 'set
things right'. To be deeply, utterly at peace. This is
the outcome of discovering how precious life really is. Beyond the simple beauty of a robin's solitary song or a child's laughter, a person senses that
there is a meaning and purpose to that very life.
Life isn't a random thing or an incidental. It is full
of truth. A dying person suddenly sees that life is
so much more than making plans and fulfilling
ambitions. So much more, even, than reaching out
towards certain important goals. Life is centred in
God. It is the overflow of his fullness. And each
life can only have meaning, can only know true
fulfilment, when it lives in such peace and harmony with its source that it can, at last, be taken
fully back into him from whom it first came.

It is then, in the light of this new understanding, that a person suddenly knows he must consider things which perhaps never seemed important before. He must get them clear in his own
mind, and then apply them to his own immediate
situation. To stop short at anything less would be
to deny himself all the rich fulfilment for which

he was made, and into which God longs to finally welcome him. It is a tremendous moment of recognition, a climax to his whole life.

Some – like Simon or Dr. Casson – will already have known such a moment. That sudden realization that they were not yet at one with God and in harmony with him, because the wrongness of their hearts and lives made such a oneness impossible. But then, with great wonder, they had asked for and found forgiveness, and restoration through Jesus' deep love in dying for them. He'd taken upon himself the punishment that should have been theirs, and so the wrongness could be completely removed and the full joyous harmony could become possible. A harmony which made heaven not only a hoped-for reality, but a certainty! And which, even now, gave them a whole new viewpoint on their own suffering. Jesus was with them in it all, understanding fully, even as he had so fully suffered. Dr. Casson wrote:

Our Lord is not standing by seeing how we get on, he is actually suffering with us. Our pain is his pain, our swollen useless limbs are his, but ultimately our weakness becomes his (imparted) strength and our defeat becomes his (imparted) victory.

And, most important of all, that act of coming

to Jesus Christ for forgiveness and for complete restoration makes so close a oneness possible that a person is 'taken back into God'. He is safe both now and for always. It is a total security – a most wonderful truth! Although the fear of physical dying (so normal a fear) may still remain, there is now no longer any need to feel apprehensive about what may lie beyond death. For, to the person who is already at one with God it will be 'but the beginning of something far greater.' Something far more full of richness and delight than any picture our ordinary human minds can begin to imagine. What a tremendous certainty this is!

This certainty holds the most significance of all for someone who is approaching death. This, of every hope, is the highest, and one to which people like Simon and Dr. Casson and many others can cling with complete confidence. It will never, as every other lesser hope, be taken from them.

So we who have found safety with him (God) are greatly encouraged to hold firmly to the hope placed before us. We have this hope as an anchor for our lives. It is safe and sure, and goes through the curtain of the heavenly temple (Hebrews 6: 18-19 GNB).

My mind has been drawn to Simon's words –

words which struck me with force even as he first said them:

'I definitely still believe in a God of love, despite my illness, because it is all leading to something really big in my life.'

I didn't interrupt and ask him what he meant because I sensed that he wanted me to hear between his words and understand that this was his way of expressing this greatest hope of all. Through the tender love of Christ, through the power of his forgiveness, through the deep wonder of now 'belonging to him' – as Simon put it – he could not really die. Instead he would most definitely go on to something really big in his life, to the rich fulfilment towards which, even in his darkest days, he had still been progressing.

If ever there could be an answer for the extreme anguish of dying and death, it must be this. And, of all people, it was a young dying lad who underlined this truth for me, speaking with such certainty and conviction that his words will always remain firmly in my mind. This certainty was all he had left, but it was also all he would ever really need, for it reached far beyond his suffering into a whole new world.

As I write now I can look out over the river and leafless trees, across the white fields and pinewoods towards Bennachie. Snow is falling again. The winter is far from over. But my eager hope and expectation of spring will not be disappointed. One day the lark will rise again into a gleaming sky. One day wild daffodils will follow the first snowdrops, and bluebells fringe the old mossy road beyond the Don, each offering fulfilment for my hopes. And one day Simon's greatest hope will also be fulfilled. The *something really big in my life* for which he longs so much.

Chapter Six

Ordinary life in the light of death's certainty

'Who can know how long his life will last?'

My interest is in the future because I am going to spend the rest of my life there. (Charles Kettering)

All your life an unattainable ecstasy has hovered just beyond the grasp of your consciousness. The day is coming when you will wake to find, beyond all hope, that you have attained it, or else that it was within your reach and you have lost it for ever. (C. S. Lewis, *The Problem of Pain*)

Very old real Christians get beyond ministry. Whatever it is they've got to have at the end, it is waiting to be found inside them. (A matron of an old people's home in Ronald Blythe, *The View in Winter*)

Teach us how short our life is, so that we may become wise (Psalm 90:12 GNB)

It has been a magnificent, almost springlike day! The last drifts of snow have melted away in the warm eager sunshine, and the grass beside the Don is a vivid green. How welcome the colour seems after so many weeks of endless white and grey! At present there's a swift current on the swollen river, its brown water rushing over the boulders and sweeping on past banks of old crushed reeds. On the further side I can see the first faint haze of green and soon clumps of wild daffodils will unfold and dance to the March wind. I keep looking for them!

There are snowdrops everywhere – thick tufts of them over in the woods. I've never seen so many crowded together before, frail and yet determined to push up through the cold, frosted earth.

This afternoon thin clouds were brushed out against the blue sky and somewhere across the fields a skylark rose, full of song. What a wonderful sound! Spring really is ousting old tired winter at last! There's an eager expectancy in the air and we're more than glad to forget the deep snow and the hazardous ice. Easter itself is only a few weeks away!

This evening I cycled over the ridge, past the dark churchyard, and a little way up the further hill. I'd arranged to spend an hour or so with our church beadle, eager to find out more about village life and his own long-standing family con-

nections with the community here. What a fasci-
nating evening it proved to be!

His parents' home lies just beyond the churchyard, almost within the shadow of the small kirk.
Beside the long, low homestead is a joiner's workshop which once provided for a variety of needs
in the small farming community. 'Everything from
the cradle to the grave, literally!' the church officer told me as we chatted together. I asked him if
his father and grandfather really did make cradles.
'Yes, and many other items besides, mostly for the
farms. Cartwork was an important part of a day's
work, but it all came to an end after the war. It's
over now.'

'What do you do instead?'

'Well, in the seventies we worked on several
old stone cottages which were being rebuilt out in
the countryside by some of the newcomers in this
area. Now we're doing more home joinery here in
the village.'

He showed me an old photograph taken in the
early 1890s. 'See, there's the blacksmith's, close
to the joiner's workshop. Both were needed by
farmers. Our family would build the carts and he'd
make the wheels. Farmers brought their horses to
him to be shod too. Plenty of work!' The beadle
had mentioned coffins, and I knew that he and his
father were also the undertakers in our village.

'Do you still make coffins?' I asked.

'No, they're bought from the city now. Chipboard with a veneer. Nothing like the heavy wooden coffins we once made here.'

We sat together in the warmth of his living room while a tall sonorous grandfather clock ticked and struck from its corner. (A young grandfather, in fact, 'I made it last year!') A sharp wind had blown up outside and sometimes it angrily flung itself against the window. I asked about an undertaker's life.

'Is it hard to work outside in the cold northern air, particularly when the winter is so long and tiresome?'

'You get used to it. It's not something you think about too much!'

'How many funerals are there in a year?'

'It's very variable. Forty, two years ago. Twenty-four last year. Mostly older people. The newer families here don't often ask for help. They call an undertaker from elsewhere. Younger people seem to find death very disturbing. They want the person who's died to be taken out of the house as soon as possible. There's no room for death in their small modern homes. Older people are different. They have grown up with death. Seen it. Death was common when they were young. It happened to everyone; babies, children; young parents. Everyone. They didn't find it as disturbing as people do now.'

'Is it difficult being an undertaker in a village

where your own family has grown up alongside generations of almost every other established family? Does it seem like a personal loss?

'Yes, 95% of the people whom I bury are my friends. You have to conceal your emotions.'

He smiled a little. 'A newcomer once commented that I couldn't possibly be the village undertaker because I looked too cheerful. But one has to wear a face to suit different occasions.'

We talked on and on. I could have listened for hours, but it was getting late. I stood up and began to put on my scarf and coat. The church officer paused for a moment, then he said, 'Everyone needs to think seriously and carefully about death. But few do. It's going to happen to everyone, but they just let time go on passing by as if death didn't matter.' He stopped for a moment. 'But some are ready. Older people mostly. "You'll find everything in an envelope on the mantelpiece," they say. They're just waiting for death to happen.'

Then he went on to tell me about some memorial stones which had already been set up in the village churchyard even though the people whom they commemorate were still living. 'They arrange for the stone to be erected in advance with their name, date of birth and village address already inscribed. Then there's a blank at the bottom where the date of death will be written later.'

I was surprised, having never heard of such detailed pre-planning before. I was also interested in the church officer's comment about everyone needing to think seriously and carefully about death, whatever age they might be. I remembered that November morning many months back when I lingered beside Calum's grave and began to consider different facts and questions about death which had never really occurred to me before. They had stirred me deeply, and the more so when I realized that I, too, would one day face death. I would enter into that experience which Calum had already, so tragically, known. That morning I began to sense the urgency of fully facing up to death's certainty, and then living an entirely different kind of life in the light of that fact. The thoughts are still with me, made even more real now since meeting and talking with people like Edna, June, Eileen and Simon. They have each, in their own way, underlined the beadle's words.

What I particularly noticed was his emphasis on 'everyone' and it made me realize that every person's life is linked with death. Death is the one certainty which everyone faces. I can see that older people are more likely to think seriously and carefully about death because they are increasingly aware that life is nearing an end. All along they have taken care of various practical details relating to life, and now many of them feel urged to do the same regarding death. All kinds of different

arrangements start to go through their minds;
thoughts of who will sort out their home, how their
possessions are to be distributed, what hymns they
would like at their funeral, and where they will be
buried. Perhaps too, they will even choose their
own memorial stone. They begin to get ready to
leave even though there is such sombreness in
doing so. One eighty-six-year-old lady said:

*My day has quite gone. It is over. Quite gone ....
What I have complete faith in is that there is another life. I've got total faith in that. I don't hesi-
tate at all. So there is a greater experience soon.
Everybody is going on the same journey .... I don't
say that I'm prepared to die. But I am prepared to
leave. I've got everything (material) arranged. But
whether I myself am prepared – that's a very different matter.* (From Ronald Blythe *The View in
Winter*)

That older lady's words were so full of openness and honesty that I immediately felt drawn to
her. The fact of death was put clearly, without any
cover-up. She was meticulously prepared to leave
– I've a feeling that she must have been an organized person throughout her life – but as to whether
she was prepared to actually die, 'that's a very different matter'. I realized that her words were point-
ing to a definite and interesting distinction. She'd

got everything around her ready but she wasn't quite sure whether she herself, as a person, was ready. That aspect of death was still on her mind. It had yet to be resolved. And being a careful, open person it probably soon would be!

Her frank admission of uncertainty on this point has reminded me of another lady – older even than eighty-six – who lives quite close to us here. Her whole way of looking at life shows that, in contrast, she has already resolved this question. As a person she is ready for death simply because she is already completely at home with God. In giving herself fully to him, she has come to really know him, just as if he were sharing her small house and entering with her into this long evening time of her life. She is his, and he is hers! And, despite her frailty and increasing physical weakness, the reality of this friendship with God often shines in her face. Jesus' own words express this being 'at home' with God very well:

If a man loves me, he will keep my word, and my Father will love him, and we will come to him and make our home with him (John 14:23 RSV).

I first met Miss Emily (that is the name I will give to her) soon after we arrived here in the village, and she has since become very dear to me. There is a real bond between us. Recently we found ourselves sitting next to one another at a Sunday service and I saw that Miss Emily didn't need her hymn book for any of the hymns, even those which were less common.

'You seemed to know every single hymn by heart!' I commented afterwards.

Miss Emily's face lit up. 'Aye, of course I do. I've sung them all my life!' She paused for a few moments, letting her mind reach far back over the years.

'When I was still small my mother would say, "Rock your baby brother to sleep!" So I would sit and rock his cradle – it was a wooden one which the minister's wife gave to our family when her own bairns had grown – and while I rocked him I sang every hymn I could remember.'

There was another silence, and then Miss Emily went on.

'And I still sing them. My eyes aren't good now – it's like a mist – but I don't need to read the hymns. They're inside!'

We talked on for a little while, Miss Emily taking my hand in hers. Before we parted she looked up into my face and said earnestly, 'I wouldn't be without my hymns, nor my Bible. What would life be like without them? What would it be like without God?' and she shook her head slowly, as I know she always does at serious moments.

In being at one with God, often enjoying him,

Miss Emily has found a way of overcoming any fear she might once have had about death. It is no longer a hushed-up subject but rather an event to which she often refers. Not in a morbid way, but with a simple expectancy. She talks of death as 'going home' and by her use of the word 'home' I've understood that she sees death as uniting her even more closely with God, so that it has now become a happening to be welcomed rather than dreaded. That's not to say Miss Emily isn't apprehensive about the actual moments of dying. I imagine that she must sometimes experience this natural and normal fear. But any such apprehension is comforted by realizing that death will merely be a final step bringing her to the very doorway of heaven.

One morning we spoke at length about life after death because Miss Emily seemed to have the matter particularly in mind.

'Aye, but I *hope* I shall go to heaven!' she said, a little wistfully. (I think she was afraid of being presumptuous.)

'Do you say 'hope' because you don't know if you ought to be sure?' I asked.

'Yes, I'm feart to be sure. Can anyone be sure?'

I paused, wondering how to answer. 'Didn't Jesus promise that those who'd been forgiven and were now at one with him would go to join him in heaven?'

'Aye, he did!' she answered firmly.

'Then we can be sure because he wouldn't tell us anything untrue!'

Miss Emily thought for a moment, and nodded. 'Yes!' she said. 'Yes, maybe we can be sure.'

Despite her hesitancy, I knew Miss Emily was sure of heaven. Her very joy at the thought of it gave proof of this. And our conversation about heaven's reality made me even more aware of the urgency and importance of considering death and its outcome. I can see now that it isn't just a relevant matter for elderly people. The undertaker's emphasis on 'everyone' was the result of his recognizing how everyone faces the certainty of death even while they still live. He had buried people of all ages, knowing the intense sorrow of sudden unexpected bereavement and the poignancy of a young person's dying, as well as the quiet 'going on' of older people. It was inevitable that he should caution everyone to be ready.

The undertaker was referring to practical readiness, whereas my thoughts have also centred around personal readiness. But, for all the advisability of this, such thoughts are bound to be difficult and unwelcome. Who wants to consider the matter of death when they are still young and strong: when there is yet so much to live for? So much to anticipate and plan?

Our natural human reaction to the unwelcome

certainty of death is to concentrate our thoughts on here-and-now ambitions instead so that death will automatically be programmed out of our thinking. Before long it becomes a silent, hushed-up subject which we avoid in conversation. But deep within ourselves we know this is a pointless way of dealing with truth. It will not be eliminated simply by being ignored. Instead the certainty of death will only appear the more baffling when circumstances suddenly force us to come face to face with its reality.

I remember how moved we all were at Calum's funeral. There were several of his young friends present, fellows who might previously have seemed casual about death, even indifferent. But there in the churchyard the reality of the coffin, and the wreaths and the anguished parting touched us all very deeply. I'm sure that many of us were inwardly changed. We began to look at death in a new, disturbing way.

And it was essential that we should see it so, for such a recognition becomes the first step to being personally prepared for death. It isn't in any way a morbid response, but rather the only sensible way in which we can react to so solemn and certain a truth. If we know that something momentous is definitely going to happen, then we are immediately stirred into making preparations for the event. And nothing could be more momentous than leaving this life behind and going into all that lies ahead. We daren't not be ready, for the risks are too great.

But even when we reach this point of sudden urgency it is all too easy to stall. To hold off. Maybe this was another reason why our church officer was so emphatic on the matter. He knew that people needed to go on beyond just thinking that preparedness was advisable to actually being prepared, and in this way finding reassurance for all their previous fear. I think that this must be the turning point of the whole question, that upon which all else depends. For to know that we ought to do a vital thing and then to put off doing it, is eventually to be held more responsible than if we'd never even considered the matter in the first place. And certainly it is to miss the deep rest and peacefulness which we could otherwise have known and enjoyed. Then too, there is particular wisdom in acting on a firm conviction straight away, if only because the opportunity may not be presented again.

Teach us how short our life is, so that we may become wise (Psalm 90: 12).

It is true that our lives are – as far as anyone can gauge – only as long as they have become today. The rest is completely indefinite. Thinking of it this way has made me realize how crucial today is. Today I must know beyond all doubt that I am at peace with God – or if not I must kneel before him in genuine humility and become so – for I cannot know if tomorrow will offer any further opportunity for oneness with him. Today I must live in responsiveness and love towards God, for I cannot know if I will be offered that rich privilege tomorrow. I must not miss all that today so magnificently and so decisively offers. The loss might be too great. It might even mean the loss of heaven itself.

Last week a friend phoned me up in great excitement and said, 'I've found peace with God at last! I've come to him through Jesus!' It was a joyous moment of sharing together. I hardly knew how to respond. My words seemed so inadequate for what I really wanted to say. We chatted for a few minutes, our different comments full of a new happiness.

'It's wonderful to know that my whole life is safe now,' my friend said at one point. 'Even if I were to die it wouldn't be the end. I'd go on to heaven. I can't think how I could have waited until now without getting that one vital point straight. It makes me shudder when I realize that until yesterday, when I gave myself fully to Jesus, I wasn't really safe at all. I couldn't have gone to be with him in heaven. The unforgiven parts of my life would have made it impossible for me to live in a perfect place like that.'

'It sounds so clear-cut, put in that way!' I commented. 'Almost as if you've stepped from death into life!'

'Well, that's true. I have, haven't I?' my friend answered.

Our conversation together made me stop for a little while and consider the alternative to heaven. It came as a solemn realization. If death is a no-no word, then any thought of hell is definitely unacceptable to many people. The idea is so frightening that, as with death, our instinctive reaction is to programme hell out of our thinking, or else to comfort ourselves with the thought that a God of love would never want anyone to go to such a place. In a way that is true. God certainly wouldn't want any of the people he's made and loved to go to hell. He loves them too much to want such a terrible thing to happen to them.

But, at the same time, people condemn themselves to hell by deliberately refusing to come humbly and fully to God, with a genuine desire to love and obey him who already loves them so much. It is then, by their very attitude of indecisiveness or indifference, that they inevitably set the direction of their lives away from heaven and towards the only alternative. Nothing could be more full of sorrow or more tragic. How much such an attitude must grieve God, who longs for all to enter into the safety which Jesus, by his suffering, made possible to us. As the disciple, John, once wrote:

He who believes on him – who clings to, trusts in, relies on him – is not judged ... But he who does not believe is judged already; he has already been convicted ... because he has not believed on and trusted in the name of the only begotten Son of God (John 3:18 Amp.).

Jesus confirms the fact of hell: see such verses as Matthew 10:28; 25:46; Luke 12:4. He taught this truth so that we might be careful to commit ourselves to him and so be saved from hell. It is also important to realize that only God can accurately know a person's heart. Many have turned to him in the closing moments of life: the crucified thief was one (Luke 23:40-43).

One of the most exciting truths of all is that in coming fully to Jesus, as my friend had just done, we enter into a completely new way of here-and-now living. Life really does have a whole new dimension! We begin to see everything through new eyes, whether big, important issues or simple, everyday circumstances. Then too, we're not alone any longer but living alongside God, living with him in fact, for he has moved in to share our whole life. That's not to say, of course, that each day will now flow peacefully along, but it does mean that when difficulties and setbacks occur (and there may be even more now than before) we have immediate access to all the tenderness and understanding, all the constant support of a God who lives with us, and to whom our lives are totally committed. We can hand over our bewilderment to 'higher authority' and know, with certainty, that he has all our concerns under control. And so there is no more frightening aloneness in our difficulties and sorrows.

Let him have all your worries and cares, for he is always thinking about you and watching everything that concerns you (1 Peter 5:7 TLB).

It's interesting to see how all kinds of ordinary, everyday situations are seen through new eyes too. Our Monday to Friday work becomes something to be shared with God; and about which we can talk to him asking for particular patience, wisdom or physical strength. We suddenly see that it is being done for him even more than for an employer, and this makes us the more eager to carry it out well.

I've often enjoyed the story of Brother Lawrence, a Carmelite lay-brother who lived in the seventeenth century and who spent some time as cook in the busy monastery kitchen. In a small book about him, *The Practice of the Presence of God*, there is this paragraph:

Brother Lawrence had found such an advantage in walking in the presence of God .... It was observed that in the greatest hurry of business in the kitchen, he still preserved his recollection and heavenly-mindedness. He was never hasty or loitering, but did each thing in its season, with an even uninterrupted composure and tranquillity of spirit .... 'In the noise and clatter of my kitchen,' said he, 'while several persons are at the same time calling for different things, I possess God in as great tranquillity as if I were upon my knees.'

What a person! We may dismiss his example as being 'way above me' but I'm not sure we should do. Such tranquillity in his busy kitchen became possible to Brother Lawrence simply because he longed to stay close to God in his work. And God rewarded his longing with his calm presence, even as he is glad to reward us all, if only we long for him enough.

That same close oneness with God enables us to look at those around us with new eyes too – a marriage partner, our families, friends, neighbours, work colleagues, those in particular need. We recognize that they are also deeply loved by God and that he can therefore give us his love for them even

when, humanly speaking, we find them quite un-
lovable. Love can come to us as much from willing to love as from feeling loving. In fact, a willed
love may be far more stable and effective than a
felt love. If we set our will to love someone and, as
proof of this, ask God to love his love through us,
then the whole relationship does change.

It is because we have now begun to look at that
person from God's viewpoint rather than from our
own, seeing him or her as someone whom God
made and for whom he cares. Someone who mat-
ters very much to him and who can therefore come
to matter very much to us. This is not a cold grit-
your-teeth-and-do-it thing, for the will to love is
rewarded by feelings of love. And feelings of love
bring us joy. To love another person is, in fact, to
express our love for God, whereas to continue in
ill-will is to eventually bring a professed love for
God into question.

Another aspect of this new, fulfilling relationship with God has been much on my mind too,
particularly since reading Dr. Casson's booklet, *Dying, the Greatest Adventure of my Life*. It's the
matter of career ambitions and long-term planning.
They're still important but they don't fill the whole
screen any longer. Other considerations now seem
important too: how do these different ambitions
fit with the fact that, compared to eternity, my life
here is so short? If I attain them will they still count

when I go on into eternity? Will I be glad about them, or will I wish that I had worked towards higher, more lasting goals? Goals which gave pleasure and honour to God?

This is so important an evaluation. Dr. Casson emphasized these points, recognizing that his professional work, personal ambitions and day-to-day aims – in fact his whole way of living – would be assessed as important only if they could be offered back to God with humble confidence on that day when death brought him to the very doorway of heaven. No other scale of priorities really mattered. Nothing else must draw him away from true, eternal values.

Inevitably this also affected the way this young seriously-ill doctor looked at possessions. As he himself put it, 'We are going on a journey and not one item can go with us.' This conclusion on the matter didn't mean that he gave everything away and lived in virtual poverty (as a man with pressing family responsibilities that would definitely have been an unwise over-reaction), but it did mean that such items as a lovely, well-equipped home or a new car didn't seem nearly so important after all. They now began to assume their rightful place far down on the new scale of values which God was showing to him.

So many different, valuable changes come into our lives as we become more and more at one with

God! I've only mentioned a few, but each day and week will bring more. The effect is total. And it is totally good, without any regrets. Rather, there is a strong sense of well-being and of complete security. A tremendous new joy! In so living with God we find ourselves coming to love and cherish him more and more, entering into deep happiness even now.

And, more than all else, through this valuable oneness we are drawn from the bewildering, superficial surface of life to its very centre. In possessing God, and being possessed by him, we find ourselves one with the very source of all that is good and true and beautiful, all that is lasting and therefore all that will ultimately matter. We are completely provided for, completely prepared!

At the end of his long busy life Richard Benson, founder of an Anglican order called The Cowley Fathers, expressed this 'possession of God' well. Although he was speaking as an old man, about to enter heaven, this same wholehearted devotion is asked of us all. To live centred in God is our highest privilege and joy!

If I find no home any longer in this world, it is because God has been withdrawing me, my love, my treasures, my remembrances, my hopes, from a place where the frost-wind of death touched every precious thing .... I must begin to long for home. I seem almost asleep, but my heart is awake. Memory sleeps, action sleeps, thought sleeps, but love is awake. It does not think, or plan or labour to remember, but it loves; it is withdrawn from the surface of life to the centre.

Conclusion

**'Because I live, you will live also'
(John 14:19 RSV).**

Our hearts ache, but at the same time we have the joy of the Lord – and I realize that the joy is greater than the ache. (Words of a young widow – mother of twelve children)

For love is eternal and life is immortal and death is only an horizon, and an horizon is nothing save the limit of our sight. Lift us up strong Son of God that we may see further. (Attributed to Bede Jarett)

Christ in you, the hope of glory (Colossians 1:27 RSV).

Just as I was nearing the end of writing this small book we heard sad news. Simon had died. I knew he'd been steadily weakening, but eventually double pneumonia necessitated urgent re-admission to hospital. He lived only a few more hours.

In those moments of bitter realization (just after a brief phone message) I felt a deep inner pain. The sudden, sharp stab of loss. And there was a strange emptiness too. I would never see Simon again on earth, never hear his eager voice telling me different hopes and ideas, never be able to send him a postcard or a letter. He had gone.

I am still trying to realize that it is true. And if I feel so bereft without him whatever must it be like for his parents? For Louise and Pete? Just a few days after Simon's funeral, Wendy phoned me:

'We were sorry you couldn't come down here to Dorset for the funeral, but we understood,' she said in a calm, straightforward way. 'It really was a remarkable service and I wanted to tell you all about it. For one thing, there were so many people. The small church was packed – it holds around 200 – and there were more friends outside. Being a Saturday, and a warm sunny one too, everyone wanted to come and show how much they cared. It meant such a lot to us to see them there. I suppose Simon really had become well-known around here through the Fund. I realize that now.

'And the service itself, well, it was a triumph!

That sounds impossible for a funeral, but it really was true. This week people have kept stopping me in the street, or phoning, and saying, "Those words, and the hymns too, had such meaning. They showed me that death isn't the end!" And they're right. Everything about the service emphasized the reality of "resurrection" even though it was also such a terribly sad occasion.'

Wendy paused for a moment, letting her mind go back over the details of the service. 'One of the ministers began by saying "We are here to give thanks for Simon's life", and that set the pattern for all that was to follow. We were giving thanks, and despite our sorrow, it was lovely to have an opportunity of doing so together. I really could sing

> *Praise, my soul, the King of heaven;*
> *To his feet thy tribute bring.*

with a full heart because those words expressed the truth of what I was feeling. We had another very stirring hymn too, one which Simon particularly enjoyed:

> *He who would valiant be*
> *'Gainst all disaster,*
> *Let him in constancy*
> *Follow the Master.*

There's no discouragement
Shall make him once relent
His first avowed intent
To be a pilgrim.

'The singing wasn't at all slow and sombre. It was loud and strong. That was mainly because the choir of Simon's school and the church choir itself both gave an excellent lead. But I also felt that everyone in the church wanted to sing. They wanted to put themselves into those words.

'I think that the last part of the funeral, at the graveside, was most meaningful of all. I suddenly realized the full, final significance of physical death. It became absolutely real. Since then I've pictured the scene around the grave over and over again in my mind. It has been hard, but it has also helped me to come to terms with the fact that Simon has gone on into another world now. He's left everything here behind, including all the suffering. It's over.

We've been to the small graveyard every day since the funeral. The flowers are still so beautiful. The cold weather this week has kept them fresh. And looking at them there I've realized how many people have been with us over these long months, and in our sorrow now too. It's a tremendous comfort. People just don't realize how much this means.

'Do you know, the undertakers brought us a special album today in which they'd listed all the floral tributes, and written out the wording of each card. They'd also recorded the names of every single person who was present at the funeral, even though there was such a large crowd.

'It has quite overwhelmed us to realize how much Simon meant to so many people. I think his life, and even his dying, will have made a real difference to some of those who knew him.

'One friend phoned me yesterday and said, "You know, those words at the funeral about Simon being sure he would live beyond death have really made me think. Important things which I'd pushed right to the back of my mind are starting to have new meaning. I want to understand them now and get them sorted out for myself." '

We talked on for a little while longer. There was sorrow in our conversation for our hearts are still very sore, but it was also mingled with joy. And our joy was only a faint shadow of the delight Simon must now know. At last he has reached that 'something really big in my life'! Wendy indicated this same fulfilment in a tribute to her son which she wrote as part of his death announcement. The simple words are very moving:

> *Most valiantly*
> *he fought to live*

and died
to live again.

* * *

At last Easter Sunday is here! A radiant day! The
whole world around us has exploded in light and
warmth and colour and joy. Sunlight gleams across
the wide sky and streams down to touch each sudden green with new intensity. Crocuses crowd the
village lawns with mauve, white and gold, and the
breeze dances with the wild daffodils along the
river bank. Today I saw a red squirrel leap from
beech to beech above the Don, celebrating his delight at freedom after so long a winter's imprison-
ment. I heard the far-off plaintive cry of a curlew
as we walked to the kirk, and close by several oyster-catchers were poking long orange beaks into
fresh furrows. The nine limes overlooking the
churchyard are bursting with new leaf buds, and
there are vases of scarlet tulips beside some of the
memorial stones.

As we walked together into the simple church,
I noticed how the golden sun lit up the pedestal
arrangement of daffodils. Listening to the bold as-
sertive notes of the organ, I felt the swell of triumph, the joy, the amazing fact of resurrection.
For us, as well as for Jesus! My mind tried to take
it all in as I sat studying the magnificent window

above the Table. Perhaps there is no greater joy than that born out of intense sorrow and pain – the very birth-point of our delight this Easter morning. The joy is not a denial of the sorrow, not even a cover-over for it. Rather, it has grown up out of the very heart of that anguish. It is the magnificent climax! And the singing (so many hallelujahs!) is an overflow of inner wonder, inner exultation. It is a tremendous joy, a beginning! The first promise of all that once we dared not even hope for.

Today we not only hope. We know! That is the highest point of our joy. As Jesus lives, so shall we. His rising beyond death makes our rising an absolute certainty – for he is even now alive in those whom he possesses, and so they can never really die. This truth won't fit into words. It is so full of wonder!

It is the final answer, the ultimate triumph. And it *does* transform even the anguish of terminal illness and the deep sorrow of bereavement. I can see that now.

'For in Jesus 'death is not a problem; it is a prerequisite. Death makes life absolutely certain.' (J.B. Phillips)

Simon was so right. This is *'something really big!'*

Bibliography

Some of the books referred in the text are
E. M. Blaiklock, *Kathleen: A Record of Sorrow*,
Hodder and Stoughton, 1980.
Dr. James Casson, *Dying, the Greatest Adventure
of my Life,* Christian Medical Fellowship, 1982.
C. S. Lewis, *A Grief Observed,* Faber, 1976.
C. S. Lewis, *A Severe Mercy*, Hodder and
Stoughton 1977.
Katie F. Wiebe, *Alone*, Lakeland, 1976.